TUMBLEWEED CHILDREN

Written by
Sharon Watters

Grosvenor House
Publishing Limited

This book is published by
Grosvenor House Publishing Ltd
Link House
140 The Broadway, Tolworth, Surrey, KT6 7HT.
www.grosvenorhousepublishing.co.uk

This book is a work of fiction. Any resemblance to
people or events, past or present, is purely coincidental.

A CIP record for this book
is available from the British Library

ISBN 978-1-83975-204-9

Foreword:

If you have sailed through your education on task, with friends and loved every minute – this book could just briefly **entertain** you.

If your children have always enjoyed school and never experienced injustice – this book will probably **explain** the behaviours of others for you.

If you have always fitted within a peer group, succeeded, and always enjoyed your many achievements – this book might **enlighten** you.

This book is really for everyone else.

Those who don't feel they are valued and never missed.

Those who have been bullied and misjudge social situations.

Those who have stood back and wondered why they just don't get it.

Don't read or listen to this book if you are easily offended because you will be.

At the point of full maturity, Tumbleweed detaches from its roots and on reaching a final resting place, disintegrates.

Prologue:

Should it matter what our history has been? No, of course not, but it does. Each one of us knows the world around us uniquely observed by ourselves, and we attribute and link what we see using the experiences unique to us. Now squeeze that into a uniform and a uniformed system and there are bound to be sparks or friction.

We all arrive at school with a five-year history behind us. We arrive free spirits with a mind ready for wonder and awe. We are not conforming units waiting to become economically profitable nor suitably consumptive so that society can profit.

If that background has been full of joy and love, then we take on the new experience with willing compliance, but if our history has been violent or void of attention then we arrive with fear or confusion and we will not know the accepted social rules.

Born at home and never registered, John didn't apparently exist. John has five years of experience, but no one person has his full picture. It might have lacked love, but it did lack care. There may have been some joy, but the courts have decided that the care system can do a better job; give the boy a chance.

John shares his experiences with you so that you may try to understand someone else like John. He tells his story and talks directly to the audience. As he gets older, the lessons get harsher and the consequences more extreme. What will he achieve as an adult?

From John:
(For many of my early years I was not aware of being different; I am still not sure that I am. I do not remember my birth parents, there have been so many parents with good intentions who have paved the way to my current situation. I was given the label 'John'. I know that it means me and that I am alone.)

All characters and educational settings are fictional. If I wrote the truth you wouldn't believe it.

Acknowledgements.

To Maxine, Lynne, Lynda, Lisa, Helen, and my beautiful nieces who have so generously read my various attempts to write this tale. They have found the technical errors and have honestly fed back how the content has made them feel. I thank these busy women for their time and kindness with all my heart.

To my husband, thank you for your patience. x

Chance 9

It will probably be cold tomorrow. We continue to live in our rural idle. Living in such a rural location, we can feel nature's rhythms and tonight there is a marked change, it is rapidly getting darker and colder, but we are prepared for the longest night. Our reward for being a bit chilly will be a spectacular view of the cosmos. Tomorrow is 21st December and we all begin our tilt forward towards the sun and the promise of warmth and light.

We have chosen to leave all social media to those who care what others think and I am lucky enough to spend my days with every member of my family. We have no use of a timepiece or clock as our family routines matter more to us. We have chosen not to add to the high energy consumption which contributes to global warming; we don't drive cars, fly in planes, (although one of us thinks she can fly) nor do we need wireless devices to operate our home.

(I am proud of how we consider our environment.)

We know today's date because I have been following the advent calendar display in the department store windows. Twenty-five brightly coloured boxes are scattered across a floor of fake snow, each with a glittered number on the front face. One gift is revealed each day, helping those without our advantages to make decisions about what to purchase for their loved ones. We do wonder who will open box 25. Will someone miss their family meal to come and open it? Who will see it on the 25th? What will it reveal? Will the folk who live in the doorway be warmed by it?

We have collectively considered this. Jake thinks that it will just reveal, 'Merry Christmas', Miley believes it will read, 'Happy birthday Jesus', Riley says that it should just say, 'Thanks Suckers!' None of us want it to state, 'SALE' but it probably will.

We aren't purchasing gifts for each other, but we are planning a good meal. I have stored some steak for some of us. We don't usually eat much meat but it's going to be a lovely treat. Stacey, my friend, taught me how to cook it on hot stones.

(Very trendy apparently.*)*

I am also planning to prepare some braised vegetables and have bought a bag of nuts for all to share.

It has been a peaceful day today despite the cold. We miss the yellow coats, especially Stacey. I had spent much of my day remembering the happy summer we all enjoyed. Those days with twelve hours of sunshine warmed my heart.

As always, the family are going through their individual evening routines.

Riley rests at the rear of our home. He has his own spot, never tidy, but clean. He roots around until his bed is perfect and then nods off. Miley, on the other hand, always has a last-minute burst of energy and bothers each one of us and then just stops, leaving the rest of us ruffled but she is kind, so we let her. The youngest of us, Warren, flaps about and always needs to be at a good distance from Miley to be willing to close his eyes. I have my best friend, Jake, next to me and we choose to sit back to back before we nod off. He likes to face the others and I like his warmth on my back. Jane buzzes around until we are all settled and then submits to sleep as if a switch is flicked.

Charlie chooses to sleep outside. He is our protector. He says that having lived outside for years he feels vulnerable locked in. I know that he is watching out for all of us, keeping guard. If we disagree with his intent, he barks out his favourite quote as if he is in a court of law. "Sir Edward Coke said that every Englishman's home is his castle. The poorest man may in his cottage bid defiance to all the forces of the crown. It may be frail – its roof may shake – the wind may blow through it – the storm may enter, and the rain may enter – but the King of England cannot enter." He is confident about it and we let him have his moments. We have heard it many times.

(We never lock the door though just in case he wants to cuddle up with the rest of us.)

We must all be asleep before *Riley* starts snoring because, brother, can he snore.

I always try to stay *awake* until I know everyone has made it home and has shared their daily trials and tribulations with me.

I gain great comfort listening to them *settle* and sleep. It's fascinating to watch their bodies gently rise and fall with the occasional judder and turn. I wonder how I look to others or whether anyone has ever watched me sleep. Do my chums watch over me? I know that they move around our home because I often wake with Riley snoring beside me and he wasn't there when I nodded off. I am still wary of him as he has a hair-trigger temper, but I know that he doesn't mean me any harm, and after all, who am I to judge?

From my vantage point I can see the lights *flicker* on in the other homes. Families playing out their own evening routines. The houses come to life opening and closing their glassy eyes highlighting the tiny occupants playing out their own nocturnal habits.

A new couple has recently moved into the *new* house to the north of our home. I can see that they have yet to open some of their boxes. They move around together like a pair of dancers. I hope that they are happy.

I have always loved the *smell* of winter.

Chance 1: Feral

"He's had extraordinarily little social interaction with other children and can be a little wild, sad case really. He was four on the 30th of August, so he is still incredibly young. He hasn't been to preschool or nursery at all."

"He'll be fine here. We are all *experienced* teachers. We all know what to do. We will make him very welcome. Will his social worker keep us up to date with details?"

"Of course. Everything will *take* its course."

A lady who smelled of cigarette smoke and strong coffee, was the owner of the first hand that gently held my hand. It was warm. She led me to a room, showed me to a space on a blue mat and left me there.

This day was the first day of my own. My first day at school with my first teacher. As I settled into the pile on the blue carpet, I looked directly into the eyes of another child. My first experience of child behaviour. He looked back at me, shuffled forward, and yelled, "I am not sitting next to smelly."

My teeth neatly and easily pierced the skin on his arm. "John, let go, let go, let go now!"

Someone was yelling but I learned quickly. Once I had released the boy, who I didn't want to sit next to because he was too loud, I was permitted to do the work set for me in The Head's Room; there weren't any heads in there, but it was very quiet. I must be John now.

(Within days, I could have anyone's flesh in my mouth during 'outside time'. Bite and I could go back to The Head's Room. Survival here was going to be easy.)

Of course, there were meetings and other people. Women in cardigans and scarves which rarely matched and men who wore brown shoes and ties with pictures of animals on them. If they got too close to me, I would taste their clothes and they'd move away. They gave me floor space, paper, and crayons whilst they spoke to each other.

"I think we can call him feral. He needs speech therapy, support from the mental health team, and a one to one support teacher. Is Social Care involved?"

They had told me that the meeting was for me and that I could choose the biscuits. They all smelled slightly too warm and all smelled of old books and pencil shavings.

(The people, not the biscuits.)

"See, see, he'll eat anything. He's an animal."

(The blue crayon was blunt, so I chewed it sharper.)

I was always glad to hear the final bell of the day because it meant that I could make my way back to my other place. The outside was always busy, and the end of the school day gave me the opportunity to weave and dodge, just brushing the arms and legs that littered the tarmac. No one ever said 'John,' so I knew I wasn't there at all. Sometimes this was my moment to breathe the real air. The air smelled bigger in the cold.

(As I grew older, I understood that each season has a scent of its own but back then it was how I felt them.)

During the first November in school, my first animal found me.

Everything in The Head's Room was changing. A tree turned up one morning and was placed in 'my' corner. I climbed it and I was dragged back down. "John, no one climbs the Christmas tree!"

I was given a box of rubbish and was told that I could decorate the tree but having never seen one before, I left the contents and the box on the floor. I did find some red, shiny string and wrapped this around my neck. It tickled my chin and I stroked it.

"No John, not around your throat." I wrapped it around my left arm, and I had my tail. Long, strong and a comfort to me.

The grown-ups seemed to get redder and louder in December and each room had a tree inside but not like the special one in The Head's Room. The songs I could hear being sung somewhere sounded different and, boy, were they singing them too many times.

(Of course, you all know that Christmas was being celebrated but I had never known a Christmas and really didn't understand the rules.)

It was a Friday when all those people came into school and I had to sit in the school hall and not in The Head's Room, I should have been left there, I was not calm. I could smell the warmth, but without any breeze it was too heavy. The woman who had given me the box of rubbish, was talking to everyone in a purring way. I rubbed my arms and licked the back of my hand. I pushed both shoulders up and rubbed my ears. A small purr came out of me and I focussed on the purring lady. It was just me and her in that hall, warm and purring. My cat was happy and would have stayed just on that seat at the back of the large room, but the smell changed, and I pricked.

The pine needles had warmed up and were reaching me, catching on my purr. I slowly shifted my gaze to that big tree. I could see the whole thing. My purring became deeper. Near the top, tangled with some shiny blob was my tail. My beautiful shiny red tail. My tail from the box of rubbish next to my tree!

I was elegant and swift. All four limbs sprang me from my seat. Getting to the tree was just like the end of the day joy. A tunnel of space appeared before me as I pounced across the shoulders of the others in the room. They propelled me faster and faster towards my tail. Claws out and ears pricked back, I ripped up those branches dragging my scarf towards me.

My tail twisted me around and I leapt back to Earth, proud of my tail rescue.

"John! John! John!"

(Why do some people shout in threes?)

She was spitting as she finished screeching my label. She sprayed every time she screamed at me, so I did the only thing I could do, I wet myself in submission and curled up on the floor.

(These people taught me well. Piss yourself and people leave you alone or at least stop yelling. I have stopped using this technique, but I bet it would still work.)

"John is feral and it's not surprising given his background. We have tried everything, and we want him to try another school. Is his home still being watched? Has there been an investigation? Has he seen the mental health team? Can someone make a health referral? Are the new foster parents coping?"

"I think that we need to give him more time to settle in and therefore I am recommending that he stay here whilst more assessments are carried out. After all, we need to offer some stability."

Another room full of the pencil people and more biscuits. I had chosen pink wafers this time. They'd given me a pencil, a sharpener, and a dictionary. Feral – wild, untamed, undomesticated, untrained. Was that me? But I am John. I can read and write, climb, and run, I work in The Head's Room and I am warm. I pushed my paper and books out of the way curled up and drifted off to sleep.

(Well, that was the first term over, 44 to go and I am not quite feral yet!)

Chance 2: Militant Brain

I preferred not to speak to most of the others. Although, there was one who spoke to me. We sometimes met under the table. She liked to try to hold my hand, and tried to make me eat pretend food, but she smiled all the time, so I liked her and let her sit under my table with me.

I had a new person at school, he said that I could call him Steve. Steve smelt like sweets, so I didn't think that he was a smoker. Steve said that phonics are small units of sound. Bloody phonics. Everyone was doing something with 't', not 'tea or tee' but 't' for toad; again! I'd like to have told that woman that I got it but that would have meant talking to her and I simply didn't know her well enough. Toads can sit very still. I wondered what toads ate for their supper. Did all toads eat the same thing? What would they smell like? How did they feel?

(Just in case you are anything like me. I didn't mean how are they feeling today? What are they sad or happy about? I meant, if you could hold one, what texture would it have, or temperature would it be at?)

Often, Steve sat too close to me and he insisted on sitting on one of our small chairs when he was quite clearly too big. His bum hung over the sides. I knew when Steve was talking to me because he said 'John' when he wanted me to listen or move. I listened to Steve because he said 'John' before he said any other words.

When I sat under the table, Steve stayed on the chair and passed me the worksheets; sometimes I figured out what must be done and then I would return them to Steve and sometimes I just liked to be quiet and look at the books I was offered.

I didn't have to go outside with the other people, but the smiling girl, Miley, sometimes stayed and played next to me. She liked the pretend food and I like the plastic, not real, animals. I liked to group them differently each day.

There was a small aquarium at the back of the classroom. It housed an African land snail. It came into the room in the first week of school because the first phonic was 'S'. It didn't have a face like mine or Steve's or Miley's. I could write snail and, I understood that they were hermaphrodites and what that meant, I knew what they ate and where they came from, but I was still listening to 't, t, t,'. There is no 't' sound in snails.

That Wednesday should have been a calm day, Steve smelt of sugar and did not ask me if he could sit under the table with me; he knew the answer was always no. Miley was busy trying to write 't' and the school smelt of polish and not pencil, and as I said, the whole place was quiet. Steve had found me a book about amphibians and there were lots of pictures. No one had drawn in it or torn the pages, so it must have been quite new, and I was happy to touch it.

(I still concern myself with who has touched or sneezed into a second-hand book or magazine.)

Suddenly, the wailing threw everyone sideways. The wailing kept coming. Steve was saying we must go now, it's the fire alarm. Steve didn't say 'John', so I stayed on the floor. The noise went into my ears and through to the back of my eyes. It just kept coming. I put my head on the floor and tried to soak into the carpet. Be a toad, be a toad. A big hand tried to pull me from under my rock. The wailing kept screaming in my head.

"It's just a practice! Walk everyone! No one is to run! Where is that boy? Get him out!"

Steve lifted the table from over me and then lifted me up. I froze in his arms because I was too scared to move; I had wet myself again.

Outside, Miley held my hand. She smiled and started to make an 's' with her tiptoe in the dirt. I started to breathe deeply so that I could puff myself up. I licked my lips to taste the air. I couldn't smell smoke. 's' in the dirt, 's for smoke', 's for smile', 's for snail!'

My arms reached up as if to dive and my powerful hind legs pushed me forwards like the amphibian I was. The snail wasn't out! Toad to the rescue, just like Steve rescued John. As I dashed back into the building, I could hear the screaming of the others (not Steve) wanting to grab me and then, to eat me. They won't get me or the snail!

I was magnificent. Toads have such power and are so slippery that they cannot be stopped. Armed with the new knowledge that everyone must leave the building, there might have been a real fire and, no one else was going to help, it was down to me, I was going to be the one who rescued the snail.

I smashed, with one huge jump, through the doors of the building. Hopped past the room not full of heads and bounced down the blue corridor. Save the snail! I would have yelled it three times, but I only thought about it once, so I didn't; I was learning the social norms.

I grabbed the fire extinguisher and leapt into the classroom. With my powerful forelimbs, I threw the fire extinguisher at the tank and grabbed the snail. Just like Steve did with me, I held it tightly so that it wouldn't get away. I plunged back out through the now open doors. Threw up my arms and bounded out towards the screaming crowd, holding the snail in both hands.

Miley was hiding behind Steve and she wasn't smiling at me. Toad and snail needed to be away from the screaming. We both needed to be cold and wet and close to the floor.

In the garden, I left the snail to enjoy the vegetables because they eat green plants. I went under the hedge until I was very cold, and everything had stopped screaming.

(Another meeting but Jammie Dodgers this time.)

I was made to sit at the table with the grown-ups. Steve was there and brought with him books about animals, so I accepted, for a short time, that I had to sit on a chair.

"I am this young person's new social worker. I don't know all this YP's background and so I am here to listen to all the voices in the room and make a full report. Now, can someone update me on the killing of the class pet?"

"I have read that some unborn children can suffer brain damage if they become stressed. Given his background, I think that he may have developed a condition known as 'the militant brain.' I believe it can then be passed on to the next generation. Is there an assessment or test for that? He crushed the class pet to death!"

(Who had a class pet? What is a YP?)

"Can we all remember that John is still in the room and that he is very bright. It's my belief that he thought that he was doing the right thing; it just went wrong again."

"Perhaps we should consider a reduced timetable for everyone's sake. He is unable to work within a group and can only work in parallel with other children. It must be incredibly stressful for him and the others. We definitely don't like the relationship that is building between him and another child."

"The one to one tutor arrangement, clearly, hasn't worked and is awfully expensive; the school is picking up that bill y' know. We are unable to keep him safe and we also believe he is a danger to pupils and staff y' know. You know he bites and wets himself! I'm sorry Steve but you haven't been able to improve his behaviour in any way."

"I don't want to label him, but could he be suffering from Intermittent Explosive Disorder, IED. I have read about it and he does seem to fit the description, it's like Militant Brain. I'm no expert, but could it be that? Should he be tested? I don't like labels, but maybe this time."

(Have you ever noticed that people have a favourite word and overuse it? The 'but' people never want to be rude 'but' are anyway.)

"I know that I am new, but to expect foster parents to educate could lead to a breakdown of the placement. Not being toilet trained cannot be a reason to exclude any pupil, it would break the 2010 Equality Act, but safeguarding issues could be. Do we all agree that John is a danger to himself and others? Have we got evidence that he self-harms? Do we think he understands? My report will advise that John will be tutored at home until such time as a full risk assessment can be carried out."

Each one received a glancing blow as those beautiful books flew across the table.

(There are some who want to blame and others who want to solve but very few who just accept? Did anyone remember that I was in the room? It didn't matter because clever Steve had brought brilliant books that he knew I would like. Steve was moved on. Schoolwork was emailed to my new foster parents and I have never been a toad again because they aren't good at rescues. I learned all my phonics, blends, digraphs, and split digraphs, graphemes, and phonemes *without the need to repeat them twice and was a fluent reader before I was six. So, I was not feral, and I did not have IED; does anyone?)*

Chance 3: Fight or Flight

The reason for my next house move was, apparently, to experience some stability. Two dads this time; Matt and Mark. They laughed and said that they were M and M. They always followed that up with, 'Please stand up, please stand up' and then they'd stand up. I have no idea why this pleased them so much, but it did, and I learned quickly that they smiled at me if I smiled at them.

Matt always drove the orange Audi Q8 Vorsprung, without any music playing but Mark always played his music choice too loud and then sang along with it. Mark smiled so much that I could tolerate his choices and he only ever chose the same tracks, so it became familiar to me.

(Vorsprung means progress or getting a head start.)

I loved everything about autumn on the outside. I could feel warmer inside if I put my hand on the cold window. The raindrops were running down the outside of my side window but up the windscreen in the front. I wondered why?

There seemed to be more birds in the sky that day. What were they doing? I texted my last question to Matt and the Audi Q8 read my question to the quiet driver.

"They are getting ready to migrate. Some of them are flying further north where it is colder, and some are going to fly south where it is warmer. If they stay here, they won't survive because there won't be enough food for them. Some birds stay here all year long and they are called native. There will be enough food for those ones."

New words to play with always pleased me. I tried to sort them into groups as we flew past. Am I a native? Can I migrate? I am not a bird. Should I get a head start?

We were on our way to the new school. Everyone kept telling me that it would be exciting, but what did that mean? Would there be tigers or flamingos? Rhinoceroses perhaps?

(There weren't amazing animals or anything else I would find exciting. The outside world is the exciting bit. This place was just like the others but with a different floor plan.)

It smelt like the other places. Pencils, polish, and coffee. This was not exciting, and I thought that it might be too warm for me.

Matt had made me my favourite lunch this morning, so I knew that I wouldn't have to migrate to find food.

"I have read all of the documents and reports, but this is a new start for John. He will get lots of support and still be challenged. I believe that his levels suggest that he is an able child, but we will start him in a class of other young people who also find the school environment challenging. The agreed anger management training will start this morning. Won't that be exciting?"

(No answer was required here.)

"John has his lunch, and he doesn't hold hands. John prefers to text message if he has a question and he can definitely hear you."

"We have a 'no electronic devices' policy at this school so he'll have to hand in his phone or leave it with you. I realise that this strategy works for you and John, but he cannot use it here. We have a policy. Come on John, we have chickens!"

(Definitely a bird day.)

The room had a red door and a low frequency buzzing light. The whole place smelt of warm vegetables. I was greeted by a person in red shoes with, approximately, five-centimetre high heels, unnecessary white buttons, and white stitching around the edge of the toes, but I liked them. I decided that she'd be a red spotted booby. I had carried out a little research on the, twenty-three minutes, Audi journey. There was also a faded tattoo of a flower on the side of this person's leg.

Everyone in the room seemed to be doing something different and I was given a choice of activity. I didn't need to speak to these people, and they didn't speak to me, and it suited us all. I chose mathematics, multiplication, because I like multiplication patterns. There was no sign of anyone having to repeat phonics or the alphabet names; I was grateful for that. I sat calm and optimistic but I had made a judgement error.

It seemed like hell had burst open. This place had bells! No one had told me there would be bells. Did they mean fire? The bell tones scratched at my brain.

I hopped under the table. I wasn't the first to have taken cover under here as Warren, whoever Warren was, had left his name and his chewing gum beneath the surface. I thought about leaving my name but didn't have time as a huge arm pulled me from the safety of the ground.

I mustn't bite, so out of my chest came an ear piercing, eye watering screech. I obviously hit the right note and the hand released me immediately, new learning on bird day. It had however, announced to the rest of the flock in the room that screeching was a possibility and, on their migration from the room, with the bell ringing and their hands over their ears, six different birds were announcing their own displeasure by adding their own particular screech.

The room rapidly became silent, no bells, no screeching, no other YPs. I was back under the table. Red Booby with her tattoo was calmly facing out of the window as if watching snow fall.

Silently, the thinnest person that I had ever seen anywhere glided into the room; maybe she should migrate like cranes do to find some food. Where did I put my lunch? I could have asked but these old people, OPs, had a policy and that was where my phone was being held.

"Hello John, I am here to help you cope in school and get along with everyone else. I have some Lego for us to play with."

She didn't ask me to sit with her, but she did put some pieces under the table for me. Red shoes didn't leave the room.

I like Lego, but I don't like playing with other people because they try to help me build and I can already do it. They also tend to take the pieces I would like, and I have known some YPs to eat pieces; you never know where someone else's Lego has been! I was happy to watch her. Her helpless wings flapped around, and she made a small house; amateur.

"John, try to breathe through your nose and out through your mouth. You can puff up your chest and your fears will fly away. Try and do it five times. I will do it with you."

I watched her huff up and then puff out. Just watching made me calm so I tried it; it just made me think about my lunch. She passed me a red 1x6 brick.

"John, you can keep that piece in your pocket. No one will take it away. When you get frightened or worried, just look at the brick. Try it. Just look at the brick, look at the colour and the six studs on the top. Can you see the word on each stud? Look at one stud. You choose. Now look at the L on the stud. See how straight it is. Now look at the E. Focus on the middle line of the E. Keep breathing through your nose and out through your mouth John. Now look at the G, see how it curves. Finally, look at the O, feel how round it is.

"I am off now John. You keep the Lego brick and use it if you get scared. Bye for now."

She fluttered out and I could finally get out from under the table and leave Warren and his gum behind.

I needed to ask Matt or Mark whether I could take this little brick back to their house. I needed to send a message. I could feel it in my pocket, but it wasn't mine and you shouldn't take things that aren't yours because it makes OPs shout.

The Red Booby lady was standing beside the door. I didn't see her move so perhaps she can hover in those shoes. She beckoned me to walk with her and we left the room together.

The others were at a long table tucking into their lunches. The smells of bread, orange juice, milk, and ham, blending, was overpowering. I held onto my Lego

1x6 brick, I breathed in through my nose and out through my mouth like the crane lady had said. This just made the smell go deeper into my head. I took out the Lego 1x6 brick and looked at it.

"You can't have that in here! No toys allowed in the dining hall! Sit down and eat!" I held onto my brick. Crane lady said that it was mine. A huge, monstrous vulture with gravy dribbling down its breast ripped my Lego 1x6 brick from me. "It's school policy. No toys in the lunchroom! Now sit down and eat!"

Vorsprung John. I breathed in and whoosh. Migrate and survive.

I went low first and under any flailing arms. Through the door and along a corridor. Pictures on the wall were a blur. I spread my wings and touched each side. I travelled faster and faster. My feet were barely touching the floor. Big breath in and then out. My strength was building, and my speed was increasing. I crashed out through a door and into a paved yard. I startled for a moment. I didn't know where I was, but I knew where I had to go; up, up, and up.

Like a gift, there was a dirty metal staircase fire escape, waiting for me. The icy cold rail supported my bid to fly. One flight, two flights but then faced with a mesh fence. I stalled, in fear of diving back to the danger, I climbed. My wings, my beak, my feet all found purchase on that mesh and in no time at all, I was at the top, with only the sky above me.

The water on the clay tiles was warm, and as it seeped through my trousers; it soothed my inner thighs. The full ridge of the roof was like a perfect perch. Was I a native or a migrant? Should I stay on the perch or travel to my homeland?

(I loved that thrill that running free offers.)

The school roof must have been high because the others below looked so small. I couldn't determine the words being used but something had them fluttering about. The sound of their flock became just tweeting at differing pitches.

I could stretch my arms out without limitations and fold them back in to warm my chest. Breathing in with wings out and breathing out with them away. The crane lady was right, it did help me feel safer and more secure. I thought about walking along the ridge, but that would have been madness because I could have slipped and fallen. I could see for miles and the birds saw me as they flew pass.

"I warned you about that staircase. I flagged up that one day someone would get on that roof. Who should have been with him? How is this going to look to our stakeholders? If he jumps, we will all be out of a job!"

"He'll be down when he gets cold. He'll get bored before we do. Someone get me a cup of tea. I could be out here for a while and get my coat. Tell the office to phone his foster parent. Someone dig out the policy we have on this. Bloody anger management. I really don't know why we bother."

The fire appliance, that's what they call fire engines now, pulled into the front yard. Had that bell been the fire alarm after all? Was it a practice or a real fire? I couldn't smell smoke.

The appliance was quickly followed by the Audi Q8. Mark and Matt were in the front seats and I thought that I could hear a familiar song playing. Wings out and wings in. Wings out, wings in.

The twittering of the natives had stopped. They had returned to their familiar feeding ground. I imagined them at their lunch boxes. Satsumas, crisps, bread, cheese, and chocolate. I still didn't know what had happened to my lunch box, but Mark would sort that out.

I could hear the whirr of the appliance motor and watched as a ladder bumped gently against the gutter of the roof. A yellow hat followed by a fire fighter's head appeared soon after the ladder.

"Hello John, I 'm Joe, I want you to stay right where you are. Matt and Mark tell me that you prefer to talk using your phone. I have it here in my pocket and when I reach you, I will hand it over. I hope that is OK. You don't have to do anything."

The fire appliance's ladder extended and then folded and rested on the roof tiles.

"OK John, I am going to come along the ladder and pass you your phone."

Joe obviously did not know that he should not give me my phone as there was policy here, but he did it anyway. Joe handed me my phone and smiled. I liked that smile because his cheekbones went right up and backwards. It was a huge smile. He looked both confident and comfortable at this height.

"You're not in trouble."

He stayed on the ladder while I pecked at the keys.

I text Mark that I wanted to migrate and that I did not think I would survive here. Mark messaged back that if I let Joe help me down, then I could go home and have my lunch there. He was going to help me migrate.

(My new lesson, go high and go home.)

Chance 4: Autistic Spectrum Disorder

"We had hoped that this would be a multi-agency meeting, but we have had two professionals send their apologies already. His social worker will not be here as she is currently on 'long-term sick' and the speech therapy department is very stretched and has requested that we send them the minutes. Can we begin? This is a mainstream school and I am extremely busy. I can only give this matter twenty minutes."

"I have read all the assessments and I am sure this YP will be able to access his learning here. He will require a visual timetable so that he can understand his day ahead and someone can teach him how to communicate non-verbally. He is not an elective mute according to the specialist and so shouldn't be having speech therapy. I have read that the latest behaviour management strategy didn't help either."

"We can meet his needs here as we have many young people with 'additional' needs and a high staff to pupil ratio. Have there been any ASD assessments? He chooses not to speak, and he avoids positive touch. Does he have any food preferences? Does he prefer beige food? Does he make eye contact at all? I am not a specialist, but he does tick many of the boxes."

"Year six is a tricky year for most YPs during this time of transition. They are at the top of a small hill and ready to buzz off. It is the year for exams. We are taking a great risk having a new pupil here at all during this year, but I have been advised that he will attain excellent results and that is good for everyone. We are aiming for outstanding therefore I could not consider him without assurance that he'll achieve the required levels. I have my percentages to think about. We can't be outstanding without excellent percentages."

"John is our first foster child. He calls us Ann and Trevor not mum and dad. He sometimes speaks at home but never to strangers. He has had extraordinarily little contact with other children so he can find their behaviour challenging. He likes to read and is an absolute whiz at maths. He is well beyond the threshold for year six. He does worry about being safe and needs to be reassured. He doesn't like sudden change."

"Well, times up. I don't anticipate any problems. I have listened to what has been said and am sure he will fit into our routines quickly. Just email me if anyone else has any questions. I do recommend that he starts as soon as possible due to the revision timetable."

"Meeting over."

(I had been moved to Honeysuckle Cottage when M and M became mockingbirds.)

I hadn't found any honeysuckle in, on or near Honeysuckle Cottage, but there were plenty of other flowers.

Ann and Trevor were like two jigsaw puzzle pieces; they fitted around each other completely. I liked being with Ann and Trevor as they didn't make much noise. They were always busy even when they were at rest.

Ann knitted while she watched the animal programmes and Trevor tinkered in his garage and just hummed to himself. I helped Ann by holding her wool and letting it out slowly.

Trevor allowed me to sort out his garage. I had organised his screws and nails. Each type had its own box and its own specific job to do. I had labelled each type so that Trevor could hover about his work bench without wasting energy. Trevor liked me to tidy his bits and bobs.

(*His description of the tools and equipment within the garage; bits and bobs.*)

Ann liked me to help her cook and I could choose what I wanted to eat.

They both liked to be neat. They were both calm people, and no one got cross here; ever.

Ann and Trevor's neat and tidy, a place for everything and everything in its place, habitat always smelt sweet and warm. They danced around together without having to incessantly babble at each other. They had created a home that was a hive of industry, yet they were able to buzz around each other in harmony. They permitted me to join in or just watch and they both needed the routines to stay firm.

(*They liked things to stay the same. Just like me.*)

Trevor took me to school every morning in his white Ford Transit van; well, it was white once. There were small areas of rust and the whole vehicle looked like it was wearing a dirty skirt. This was probably because Trevor kept it outside throughout the year. There simply wasn't enough room in his garage for it. The rear of the van held anything that wouldn't fit in the garage yet but still might be useful one day. Those new things that didn't have their place yet.

(I would have liked to have started in the back of the van so that my own place could have been eventually agreed on.)

Ann never took me to school but always picked me up at the end of the day. Her car was yellow, old, and clean. It could have been fast, but Ann only ever drove at five miles less than legally permitted. She believed that this driving style meant that she could bimble about and be certain that if anyone stepped out into the road, she would have time to stop before killing them and therefore, keep her immaculate driving history.

(Would this hypothesis apply to a motorway?)

My new school was made of wood and had carpet throughout. Every room was carpeted a different colour and the corridors were blue. The flooring was carpet squares that link to each and could be individually replaced if they were ever damaged or vomited on. They were rough and when you removed your shoes, your socks would stick to them. It made it feel like you had Velcro feet.

(Carpets on the walls could have been fun.)

The blue stream of nylon squares allowed even the youngest member of the community to navigate without getting too lost. Anyone could follow the blue stream, if they chose, to the main hall, the toilets, the library, or another classroom. I never made any of those choices as I hadn't chosen to be here at all, but I did follow the routines and rules. It was even easier not to make a choice to navigate as I was never asked to go into the main hall; too noisy. I never use the school toilets; they stank. My room was right next to the library and I would never go into another classroom, no friends and so no invitation.

Here we were reminded, daily, that 'The whole community must work together'. Apparently, 'Everyone matters. If we all worked together then the world would be a stronger and happier place', was the plan.

I think they had a mission to develop a hive ethic without explaining the necessary jobs required. It always seemed that the days slipped past without major incidents by chance rather than design. I certainly wasn't aware of my role to contribute towards the harmony of the whole.

(Perhaps keeping out of the way did help everyone else.)

My room was warm and painted a buttercup yellow. Jane, my key worker, said it was a sunny room even on a dull day. I was the only pupil who worked in this room, but other adults kept their home things in green metal lockers stacked against the wall at the rear. They would knock and ask permission to enter and they were all very polite. They came in and left their collection of belongings and then came back in later and took them away again.

When I arrived at this school, I watched who had brought what in and who took it out again and I never saw anyone take something they didn't bring. They all seemed to be kind and calm folk. I liked them.

Jane had put a note on the door saying 'John's room' but that got torn down by one of the smallest children. There was one boy who was brought to the library, next to my room, when he was screaming. I didn't know whether the library made him scream or whether he was screaming before he got there but he screamed until his mum came to collect him.

They must have lived quite close to the school because it never took her long to arrive.

(*Or perhaps she just sat in her car outside just in case she was needed. And, perhaps he knew that and learned quickly like me.*)

Jane smelt of lavender. She was a complicated dresser. Nothing seemed to fit properly, and nothing appeared to match. Sometimes her jumper sleeves would be too long, and she would push them up making her look as if she had huge biceps. Other days she would wear a T-shirt that was too short and didn't meet the top of her trousers; I could often see her middle wobbly bit. But I was no expert on how to dress. I only wore what was given to me and never chose my own clothing. I hadn't learned how to do that yet so perhaps Jane was still learning. She wore soft soled suede shoes and they made almost no sound, just as if she was not wearing any.

Jane solely worked with me. She said it was because I was special and very clever. She had a soft purring voice when she talked but she didn't often talk. She left me yellow notes stuck to my work so that I knew what to do. I left her notes on orange sticky note paper. I liked the way we communicated, and I did sometimes, very quietly, speak to her. We had agreed that I should always say good morning and goodbye just to practice my 'polite social etiquette'. Jane had taught me to use sign language for most of my other needs. She said that it was important to be able to communicate with others in some way for my own safety. I would have liked to have been able to watch us practise sign language through the window of my room. We would be flapping away and smiling. I didn't know whether anyone else in the school could sign.

I had been repeatedly completing examination papers from years gone by; past papers. I liked doing this and it took almost zero interaction with Jane. She left my timetable each day, usually the same as the day before with only subtle variations across the weeks. Whenever I finished a paper, I had the choice of activity.

In the beginning, Jane had brought all sorts of strange toys, puppets, art materials and games into my room but she quickly learned that I preferred to read reference books or research information on the internet. She insisted that I mix it up a bit. So, I alternated between my preferred choices and her suggested craft ideas.

It was the spring term and I had researched about emerging plants and animals. From my room we had seen snowdrops and daffodils emerge and bloom. We had seen birds forage for leftovers and gorge themselves on the emerging insects.

Before the Easter school holidays, Jane busied herself making Easter cards. She knew that I wouldn't want to get sticky and make artificial flowers, draw rabbits and eggs, but she was kind enough to make one for me so that I could give it to Ann as a gift. We both signed it as she was the producer although without me, she would be in class and not able to make her whole family Easter cards, so I accepted that 'we' both had something to do with the enormous production line carried out behind me.

I had finished my research on why eggs at Easter, why rabbits, why Easter, so Jane said that we should agree on a research project for the next half term, before the real exams started in May.

In that last week of school, there were yellow and orange notes stuck to the desk, all research ideas. I had finished my final practice paper for the day and sat at my desk with a book about birds. I was trying to identify the ones I could see from my window.

Everything was particularly quiet as the whole school was in the main hall watching an, 'Educational' DVD for Easter made by Disney.

As I looked and checked my illustration of the latest bird sighting and added key indicators to the chart, I could hear scratching.

I switched my head from one side to the other, using my ears like satellite dishes, trying to locate exactly where the scratching was taking place. It was not inside.

With the knowledge that only I would want to avoid the school hall, and the latest Disney DVD, I left Jane a note that I would only be gone a few minutes and that she would be able to see me outside.

I chanced a move along the carpeted corridor and ventured out. I had detected that the scratching was coming from beneath the bottom, left hand corner of my window. Not knowing what it was that I might disturb, I was careful to tread softly.

At first glance, I could see nothing. The wooden building was a greyish brown with black window frames, and I had thought that a small rodent might be trying to dig under the wood but nothing that large was obvious and the scratching was still audible.

As I moved cautiously closer, I spotted a tiny furry insect. It had a fuzzy black bottom and short wings. Its head moved rhythmically up and down, carving out a small groove, leaving a pale brown mark. I moved carefully backwards until I felt that I could turn and dash back inside the building without disturbing this newly found creature. I had found my new project. I knew nothing about this tiny creature that had happened into my school world.

Jane hadn't noticed my absence, so I was able to fold up the last note and write the title of my new project on the back of it. The new questions buzzed around my head like an excited swarm.

Over the school break, Ann and Trevor keenly allowed me to explore the outside of their home. Trevor had found an ancient magnifying glass but recommended that I only look at my chosen subjects briefly and with care otherwise I might get stung and they might get burned.

They both encouraged regular library visits and once the librarian had understood that I wasn't a lover of animals, that I was a lover of new information and the information had to be specific, she got on board and had new text brought into her library from across the county.

(She was eager to please; a diligent worker.)

I decided to take a scientific approach to my garden observation and plotted out a map. I busied myself for the whole two weeks away from Jane and my new little companion.

I learned that there were drones, workers, and queens. I learned that some were communal, and others were solitary. I learned that, no matter which type you might meet, it is only the female who will sting you. For the first time in my short life, I yearned to return to school and assess which type my little co-worker was.

My book bag bulged with all my notes and drawings. I was so excited. I almost skipped into the building humming to myself. My little learning space and Jane were waiting for me. This was the term for the examinations and putting my project together; I was so keen.

Having completed two practice papers, one maths and one reading, I ventured outside to see if my scratchy friend was still gnawing at the wood.

(Yes, a friend.)

Jane was happy enough to allow me to be on the other side of the window if I stayed where she could see me. I was happy to comply but whenever I looked up, she was reading my notes so I could have wandered off.

There, under the window, was a tiny furry bottom bobbing up and down. There are very few wasps or bees who chew wood. My friend was a Carpenter bee. They are called that because of their habit of digging into wood surfaces to make their nests.

I checked my library book and found an image of this little chum. The female has a black head, while males have black heads with white spots. I carefully looked closer and there were no spots. She was a girl. That did mean I would have to take greater care because they are the ones who can sting but only if they feel threatened.

I was glad that my new chum was a girl as the males don't live long enough to need a nest. She was going to be around the whole summer term and would build a nest to lay her eggs in. Her nest might even be right beneath my window.

Over the next few weeks my days were almost identical to each other. Practice tests in the morning and some reading, always about bees, and then in the afternoon Jane helped me with my project. Jane had really gone overboard this time. We had a wall display about the life cycle of a carpenter bee. We had a folder and she had covered it in brown fur fabric. She had even acquired a camera so that we could take photos each day and her intentions were to make a huge montage to put across the internal windows so that everyone else could learn about the carpenter bee.

May 5th was the morning of the first examination paper. I knew this because Jane had prepared a full timetable for me so that I knew what was coming up. I was well practised, and these exams held no fear for me. New signs had been placed around the school, 'Quiet', for those who could read.

I had to wait until 9am, no one must begin before then. We sharpened my pencils ready to do whatever was asked of me. Jane took me out to see my bee before the 9am deadline.

"8:50 Come on John, you must work in the hall with all the others. Jane can't come with you in case she helps you when she shouldn't. Don't worry, it will be almost silent in there. I have put a table at the back near the door for you and you can wear your ear defenders if you like."

(*I was trying to comply so much.*)

"9am and you may begin."

I looked at the familiar layout of the paper. Wrote my name in the appropriate box followed by my date of birth and the name of the school. I turned the first page and read the instructions and then turned to the next.

The hall floor was wooden, unlike the rest of the school, and very highly polished. As the teacher, no idea what her name was, moved around, her shoes squeaked a little. She was at the other end of the hall, so it really wasn't too distracting, so I was able to begin. I told myself, head down, finish and get out of here.

"You are halfway through and you have twenty minutes left."

I didn't even look up. I knew to just keep thinking about the questions. I could feel the answers leave my brain and run down into my pencil. I loved wooden pencils. A pencil scratched as you used it and you could feel your marks being made. Of course, I knew that using a pencil meant that if my work was less than perfect; I could rub it out and do it again until it was, but this paper was easy.

The shoe squeaking came closer and I looked up. My mistake. This seemed to attract the walker. She squeaked. Her furry face came alongside my cheek. My ear defender was moved backwards.

"You can't write in pencil. It says black pen. I will get you another pen."

The squeaker squeaked quickly away and then returned. She presented me with a black biro. I clamped my hand tightly around my pencil. I continued to answer the question on page nine. I felt her fingers grasp the end of the pencil and pull upwards. She wasn't going to take my pencil. I always wrote in pencil. Jane always liked my presentation when I used a pencil. If I made a mistake with a pen, I would have to cross it out and it would make my presentation look awful.

"You must use black pen."

She was now loud enough to be heard through the ear defenders. She closed my paper and simply said no. Her whole hand squashed my paper shut.

My pencil blended into my palm. It became part of me. My pencil jarred sideways, pierced through the skin between her thumb and forefinger. A tiny blob of blood oozed out around my pencil point. I could feel my exam paper beneath her hand. I retracted my pencil.

"You little bastard!"

I wiped my pencil, opened my paper at page nine and continued to complete the answer, with my pencil.

Everyone else was moved from the hall and the clock was stopped. Jane came to sit beside me. She let me finish my paper. When I finished, I went back to my room. Jane didn't say anything but laid out my project and started putting my photos into plastic wallets.

From my window I could hear my little bee friend and I was able to spot the little yellow car bob carefully into the school car park.

"He won't be coming back into my school. I should have followed my first instinct and said no in the autumn term. I have implemented a fixed term exclusion of nine weeks, that will take him to the summer holidays. I will not tolerate violence towards my staff. I have had to let Jane take leave during term as this has been too much for her."

(*Beware those who choose squeaky shoes!*)

Chance 5: Oppositional Defiant Disorder, ODD!

(That is a new one!)

"As John's new social worker, I have been overseeing John's transition from primary to secondary school. With a move into his brand-new care home, we think that a local mainstream school might be a fresh start for him. He'll be starting at the same time as all the other Year 7s so everyone will be new."

"Will he be academic enough to cope? He seems to have missed a great deal of schooling. We are an exceedingly popular school in the county. There are very few areas of deprivation, and we attract a very middle-class, white population."

"Are you saying that you think your students or staff would be racist towards John? Because it is your job to ensure that they aren't!"

"I want him to feel welcome and I will personally be his designated teacher."

"Academically, he can hold his own. He has strong mathematical intellect and has reached the abstract stage. He prefers to find the solutions to a maths problem rather than be taught a method. He will sit well in your highest group. His written work is always technically correct, but he writes with little imagination and prefers to read non-fiction. He has a reading age of fifteen, so he is well above the national average. It is the social side of school he seems to find challenging and rules are often not understood or rebelled against. We are assessing evidence of ODD."

"As head of Year 7, this all helps me suggest a learning group tutor. He is our most experienced teacher and therefore usually works with those students with additional needs. All the new pupils come with a range of test results and we are supposed to be able to predict their GCSE grades. Bloody, excuse me for my language, ridiculous, as it is during the next five years that they encounter all the adult choices that society has to offer; drugs, sex, alcohol, pregnancy, parents clearing off, bereavement, and bloody peer pressure."

"John finds the social norms hard to learn. His early records are not comprehensive and school establishments have been a challenge so far, but throughout all of that, he has been able and willing to learn and wants to learn."

(They were all wearing navy blue. Had they noticed? One of them had purchased a jacket from Hobbs. I only knew this because she had forgotten to cut off the price label; purchased in the sale.)

"I am sure that he'll find his place in our happy community, after all everyone has a history."

(Chocolate chip cookies – the biscuit selection was better at secondary level.)

Two hundred and fifty Year 7s stood across two courts marked out for tennis, netball, basketball, and hockey, each identified by colour. This might suggest to you that I had played these games but no, I had stood on the side lines of playgrounds for almost six years and you pick up these things with nothing to do.

I stood as close to the wire gate as I could without drawing attention. The fences would take me too long to scale if I needed to get out of there, the gate was the easiest place.

Eleven adults stood on long wooden balance benches, no higher than twenty centimetres from the ground, and looked out and across us all.

The adult in the middle stated that it was morning. A blanket of silence rippled backwards across the crowd of youth.

"I am your head teacher and I welcome you to your first day of the next stage of your education. One member of staff here will become your tutor group leader and each one will call out names of those who will be in your group. You must listen for your name."

(All very personal and designed to make me trust – I don't. Ever.)

I dared to look along the adult line up, saving me from making any eye contact with my fellow peers. One of these adults was going to be my next teacher. Some seemed to have tried to look professionally suited and booted, others had tried to look, 'I'm lovely, don't be mean to me and we'll be friends.' Only one of them looked like he might have some individuality, unusual in my experience of teachers so far.

I dutifully listened for my name as I was anxious not to miss it and be the only one left standing on the tarmac. The list of names was called, and I tried to work out the pattern. It seemed to be alphabetical but with the odd exception.

It was like being in a large performance of *Ten Green Bottles*. With the end of each list, one teacher dropped off the row and the list started again.

Eventually, two hundred and forty-two had walked away and I was left standing with seven others. The Head teacher and the large, calm, interestingly dressed man still stood on a bench. Had I missed my name? Was I, again, about to be vilified in front of others for being stupid?

(*I am not.*)

'Bonjour ma classe.' The pair of immaculate, two toned boots bounced down from the bench with just a flash of bright red sock. I dared to look up. The flash of new words had me spellbound.

The best tailored suit, stepped down, nodded, and walked away. My head teacher had left the courts.

The huge man beckoned all those left to move towards him as he stepped slowly towards us; still holding his list. We all met in the middle of the courts. All in, ill-fitting, it can be grown into, blue blazers and outsized backpacks.

My sole focus was now on the giant in the middle.

His list was short; Sophie Adams, Riley Boarer, Lev Bronson, John Jones, Muriel Knight, Mollie Middleton, Ben White, Morgan White. The group seemed to have little in common and I could not see the pattern, but I was glad that the group was small, and that the adult piqued my curiosity. We would be together for 'almost' a year.

This interesting man had a symmetrical face, with no harsh angles, just soft features. He sported a beard which was trimmed, oiled, and neat. It brushed his tie with each vowel he spoke. He dressed like no other teacher I had ever seen; he did not shop at Hobbs.

It was disappointing that there were eight of us, much neater if it had been seven, for Year 7. I preferred odd numbers of people so that I could stay on my own rather than be forced into working as a pair.

As we dutifully followed this character through the corridors and across another court, one of our number insisted on running ahead. He swung his arms widely and walked with a slightly bent left knee. His chest stuck up and out, and his head moved confidently from left to right. Each time he was sufficiently far ahead, approximately ten metres, our adult leader stopped, remained silent and waited for the errant soul to return to his group. This boy would then be rewarded with a slight nod of the head and a closed mouth smile. This pattern of behaviour continued until we reached a large white building with orange window frames.

Our leader announced that our new headquarters were on the ground floor on the left-hand side of the stairwell and that we were welcome to find our own way but without disturbing anyone else within the building. The, seemingly confident boy, swaggered away from us yelling, "Follow me!".

(*We did of course but only because that was the way we were all told to go.*)

The door was imposing due to the window being at adult height and therefore no one from Year 7 could have possibly been able to see in.

As we entered the room and scanned around, seven of us were static, number eight was slapping the tables loudly and then chose where to sit, on a table of course. The rest of us made the briefest of eye contact and then chose to sit on the chairs at the tables.

"Riley, you are sitting on a table." The teacher left the statement to hang in the air until, Riley Boarer, moved to a chair but scraped it loudly along the floor before he sat on it. Everything about Riley seemed angry. He had a reddish complexion, his hair stuck up at the back, and his hands were clenched.

"Bonjour. Good day. I am Mr Cheval and I am French. I teach science and philosophy to Key Stage 3 and 4. You are now in Key Stage 3. You are in a small group because you all have interesting attributes and I am here to help make your education journey safe and successful. We will meet at the beginning and the end of each day and, of course, for science."

He had made eye contact with each one of us and we stared back. I had never heard anyone speak so musically. Riley yelled, tipped the table over and left the room. He attempted to slam the door, but it was one of those fire-doors, so it just slowly closed itself. The rest of us stayed glued to our seats as did Mr Cheval.

We were asked to write something that we wanted Mr Cheval to know about ourselves. No one was asked to talk to the class, and it was a huge relief after a very demanding morning so far. I wrote that I don't like to speak out loud. After ten minutes, Riley crashed back in and sat down.

We were issued our timetable which seemed easy enough to follow as it was attached to a map. We were given a name tag so that we could be identified. Mr Cheval suggested that we walk together and begin to support each other as there weren't going to be any adults walking with us but not to be afraid to ask anyone around school for help.

And so, we were sent out into this huge school community alone. Riley ran off only turning back to swear at us.

My new class inmates were each strange in their own way which made us very alike. Lev was short and thin with a narrow face and tiny, metal rimmed glasses. Muriel walked with her head down and her backpack cuddled in her arms. She attempted to always walk behind one of us. Mollie was very immaculately presented but her skirt was much shorter than Muriel's and she had already loosened her tie and undone two top buttons. Ben was tiny and struggled to keep up. He had a blue spray which he constantly inhaled from but if looked at he smiled. Morgan kept asking each of us not to leave her behind as she had left her timetable and map in the tutor room. Sophie was dark haired and seemed mainstream; so far.

Lev and I were clearly the only ones who could read the map as we were orientating it as we turned corners and, without intentionally doing so, led the group to each lesson.

Sophie's additional need became apparent within the first lesson. When requested to stand up and tell the teacher something about herself, she dutifully stood and tried her hardest. She tried to please but the first word she wanted to say just wouldn't finish for her. She was told to sit down. The teacher scanned the room and pointed at Muriel. "You girl", she had a name tag but no, 'you girl' was how she was addressed. Muriel slowly stood. She scanned the room, still without Riley, and whispered. Muriel quietly told us all, whilst tears rolled down her cheeks, that her dad had died during the summer holidays and that she was still very sad. "Sit down." The teacher moved quickly on. Whether she had realised her cruelty or not is, I think irrelevant, but she stopped requiring us to stand up and speak and that suited me.

The lesson was then stopped as Riley burst through the door. He announced that he had got lost and threw his bag across the table on a collision course with Sophie. "Wiley!" moaned Sophie and was promptly punched for mis-pronouncing his name. This resulted in him being told to leave and go to the 'on call' room. This was a pointless request as not one of us knew where that was. Lev and I checked our map.

Lev's first huge error came when he pointed out that the time was 11:15 and according to our timetable, we should be, in fact, in maths and not history anymore. He did this again in Maths before lunch and again during the religious studies lesson. In his defence, there were no spaces between the allotted lessons to allow for getting to and from them.

During our first lunch break, Mollie left our little team and skipped off to put herself into the centre of a group of much older boys and they picked her up and spun her around. She had folded her skirt up enough that sometimes the fleshy part of her upper thigh was plainly in sight and when spun we could all see her white pants. She was giggling and squealing with delight throughout the play. On the sound of a whistle, the older, who looked like fully grown men to me, just walked away from her and left her standing alone. It took her a few seconds to recover and she pranced back over to us to begin the afternoon.

(We just couldn't see the dangers for Mollie because we were just kids.)

When at last, we returned to our tutor room at the end of the day, Mr Cheval asked for a brief outline of how the day went.

Lev confidently, but not wisely, raised his hand and shared that Muriel's dad was dead, John doesn't speak, Ben struggled to get to lesson due to his breathing problems and had wheezed all day, Sophie can't say Riley, Mollie had difficulty keeping her clothes on, Morgan can't remember anything and Riley is a bore. Probably a fair summary of the group, but his assessment of us gave Riley every bit of ammunition to torture us with, and a special focus on Lev; but it didn't seem to bother him.

The autumn term rolled forward towards Christmas with a bizarre routine much like that first day. Seven of us moved as one throughout the day, one of us wandered in and out of lessons seemingly happy to abuse any of us at any time and all eight survived the best way we could.

The bungalow, now called my home, was a peaceful one. The staff were happy to leave me to learn alone and encouraged access to the library and helped me join an online French class. This helped enormously as I could now speak to Mr Cheval on a one to one basis without others understanding or passing comment.

I dared not look forward to going back to school as that had not ended well before, but returning didn't leave me cold.

During the first half of the spring term, Mollie was whisked away by a kind looking lady in a cardigan. She had a police car escort waiting outside the classroom and Mollie did not ever return to our group.

Mr Cheval shared that although he couldn't give us any details of Mollie's case, I thought it was strange that he considered it a case, but he could share that she would now be safe and well looked after. I hoped that didn't mean that she would come and live with me.

There were strange explanations amongst other students whispered as our now odd group scuttled by, but they presented their gossip without evidence. Ben, who had lived near Mollie, said that the police had also taken Mollie's dad and older brother and that they hadn't returned either.

As the weeks trotted past, Riley really honed his behaviour towards us. He used each of our additional needs to cruelly dominate each of us, although Lev seemed impervious to his treatment. He continued to strut around the school swearing and threatening to rip peoples skin off. I thought that this was a strange threat as the image it created brought into question, how and what with? Riley did have enough about him to run if an older, bigger pupil challenged him; but it didn't ever stop or change his behaviour.

Sophie received at least one punch a day for stammering or mispronouncing his name. Ben would have his bag or inhaler taken and waved at him until he would try and run at Riley, resulting in a full-blown asthma attack, and then missing the rest of the day. Morgan had her belongings secretly taken and hidden throughout the day which made her panic and frantically look for them in her backpack by emptying the contents onto her desk which resulted in her being threatened by staff with a detention afterschool.

(Detention never happened. Who would want to make their working day longer with one of us freaks?)

Muriel suffered the taunting of, "You've got no dad!" at least once a week which meant that she would sit sobbing at her desk for the rest of the day. Riley referred to me as a frog. Apparently, this was because I chose to speak French rather than English. This never bothered me as I am not an amphibian, they have attributes I admired, but I was able to swear back at him, in French and he was never going to understand that. I had never witnessed him pick up a book written in English, so French was going to be unlikely. This power protected me along with the fact that I was much bigger than Riley, but it couldn't protect the others. In fact, because Riley seemingly could not hurt me, he would cause more harm to them.

Easter loomed and Mr Cheval took the opportunity to incorporate the melting point of chocolate into our 'properties of materials' science lesson.

We were all given written instructions to make a chocolate egg. As a group we had to risk assess the activity. This involved writing or telling the hazards of heating chocolate and working in the kitchen instead of the lab.

(There were rules, no eating in the lab; ever!)

Lev highlighted the dangers of a gas hob. Ben mentioned the benefits of using a wooden spoon rather than a metal one. He'd remembered conduction. Muriel said that her dad had loved chocolate and liked to keep it in the fridge and said this without crying. Sophie added, without hesitation, that it might burn. I offered J'aime chaud chocolat.)

(Yes, I spoke.)

Mr Cheval gently swapped the last two words around and I repeated, j'aime chocolat chaud. All eyes were briefly on Mr Cheval until he shared that I love hot chocolate and with an 'oh' from everyone, their eyes left him. The Team Cheval were used to me speaking to Mr Cheval this way and they just waited for the translation. Morgan offered nothing as she was busy trying to find her apron. Riley was wearing two aprons and shared that he was going to get fifteen Easter eggs.

We could work in pairs or alone. Riley announced that he was going to work as a pair and the only one of us brave enough to offer was Lev.

(*I always look back and wonder whether Lev had a plan.*)

The girls and I worked at our own workstations and followed the written instructions with just the briefest guidance from Mr Cheval. Lev and Riley seemed to be at odds throughout the process. One of them constantly yelling, 'I know, you vacuous fuckwit!' and the other, shouting, 'It states on the instructions that it must be done in this order; look!'

Lev tried to take over the practical process of heating the chocolate and giving the written instructions to Riley.

I am quite sure that there was just a moment of utter silence and freeze frame before the chocolate and the pan hit the window. Metal, liquid chocolate and glass burst outwards into the corridor. Mr Cheval hit the fire alarm and hell was offered an escape.

The whole school population poured onto the playground as if drawn by centrifugal force. Mr Cheval was talking into the ear of our head teacher who remained very blank.

The whole school was accounted for and told that the practice had gone well, and that everyone could go back to their lessons. There was an audible shuffling of feet just before, "Riley Boarer, with me!" came booming across the space above our heads. Everyone turned for the briefest moment and then they all, slowly, went about their own business.

When we eventually got back to the kitchen, the cleaning staff had managed to remove most of the mess and the site manager was boarding up the window whilst moaning about his workload increasing during the Easter break and the kitchen being like a pig sty.

Mr Cheval took us back to the tutor room. He wished us a happy Easter and gave each one of us a chocolate egg wrapped in coloured foil. I looked at Lev, with a look that clearly said, "What happened?" He wrote something down on a scrap piece of paper; neither of us liked to waste precious resources. Riley can't read.

(*Imagine not being able to access all that knowledge.*)

Another term over and another holiday to learn something new. Spring, new life, renewal, and resurrection. We, the inmates of the home, were treated to a zoo visit and then a farm visit; animals seemed to be the theme. The animal that was included in both zoo and farm were wild boar. On further research, I found that they are quite easy to keep because they are omnivores. They will quite literally eat anything. The zookeepers went to great lengths to explain that they have complex social groups and that the sows are excellent mothers and that all the piglets become part of a large nursery, watched over by the matriarch sow. The farmer shared that pigs are highly intelligent and can be taught to round up ducks.

(*I can't think of a single reason a pig would need to herd ducks.*)

He also shared that they play, apparently not many animals do that, and that they cast out any male adolescent that causes the group harm.

(*Interesting.*)

On our return to school for the summer term, I felt more confident. I had navigated my way through two terms without being asked to leave. Unheard of so far in my career.

With careful observation, the torture of others went on and was actively ignored. Gangs of 'like' clubbed together, Year 11 fought with Year 10. Girls with long hair taunted girls with short hair. There were toilets that only some were permitted to use and if you had to ask, then you weren't one of the permitted. Year 7 pupils did the bidding of the Year 9.

(*What was the purpose of Year 8?*)

Riley knew that we all knew that he couldn't read because Lev told him so, and you might have thought that once his secret was out, he might have softened toward those who might have helped him, but no. He became brutal. He dominated the whole group and often trapped us like prisoners using our own unique behaviours to punish us.

(*Quite clever really.*)

During the summer term we were to take part in philosophical and ethical debates. It was going to be tricky for us as a group as we were not the chattiest bunch at the best of times. Mr Cheval assured us that we could write our opinions down, in any language we preferred, sign or talk. Mr Cheval liked equity not equality.

Philosophy appeared to be the endless possibilities and ideas, and ethics, whether we should make those possibilities reality. 'Just because you can, should you?' We briefly explored genetic experimentation. I particularly liked the 'human spare part lottery' proposal.

During these sessions, Riley was able to share all his racist, homophobic, genocidal ideas learned from somewhere, but nothing written of course. Mr Cheval and Lev challenged him on every point but also offered him alternative views. These were the only lessons that Riley remained in. He could sit on a table rather than a chair and he understood only two others would talk to him.

As the term moved slowly on towards the summer, I dropped my guard and believed that I would reach the last day; my first full year.

Mr Cheval had chosen to include social ideas into our Phil and Eth lessons. We had all become a little more confident and each one of the team could now offer something without fear of reprisals. I still chose to speak in French, nobody stared anymore, they all just waited for the translation. Should we feed the poor? Seemed like a no brainer until we learned about Reverend Thomas Malthus. It made us think. We learned about the Russian revolution and the causes of social inequality.

Riley began to really engage with the group and I certainly hoped that he might stop swearing, threatening, and punching his victims. Ben, Sophie, Muriel, and Morgan had suffered most. They had just become so accepting of it as part of the day. Riley avoided Lev and would begin rooting around in his bag if Lev got too close. This didn't mean that Lev was safe, but it did give him a break from being sworn at.

One afternoon, Mr Cheval had found a DVD dramatization of a story called *Animal Farm*. Over the course of two weeks we watched a little section each afternoon and then discussed what we thought was going to happen. What were the social issues and were they ethical? We watched with interest not least because it was old school filming and looked really dated. Mr

Cheval didn't once give his point of view nor did he insist we watch for any other reason than to enjoy some quiet time together.

(Perhaps he thought that he had achieved group cohesion.)

Riley got bored first and started naming the characters with our names. He stated loudly that Muriel's dad had probably been taken to the abattoir. That Ben was next. Sophie would be cast out because she could not possibly sing the song and he would be the leader.

Mr Cheval kept trying to expand our views, ideas, and opinions but each session usually ended in someone's tears and so we moved swiftly on from the ideology of communism before someone got hurt. Lev was disappointed as he stated that if we could just get rid of the dominating, ruling individuals then everyone would feel equal.

As the end of term was on the horizon, Mr Cheval, now our valiant leader, had instilled a sense of self-belief and power into my school day. Until now, I had been a reluctant participant but with planned celebrations on the 14th of July, I was ready. No more bullying! Fete de la Federation! Liberty, Equality, Fraternity! We would all be free of the bullying. A time for parties, parades, and joy.

Tomorrow was planned in detail and we all had a part to play. Sophie and Ben had made cakes, Lev and I had been shown how to make indoor fireworks, Morgan and Muriel had made beautiful masks for each of us and Riley, with Mr Cheval's support, had planned a dance for all of us to learn. We would all enjoy ourselves and all feel like we belonged and not so odd.

I entered the last tutor lesson of the day with hope of friendship, solidarity, comradeship, and a cessation of torture for all. Mr Cheval, the hero, leader, and fellow of our team welcomed us in and told us the story of the Storming of the Bastille. He became very animated and it clearly meant a great deal to him that tomorrow went well. He was proud to be French and of France's history.

The day ended as all days had ended with the whole team leaving the room at 3:30pm. As I took my usual route across the front of the building, a glimpse of something caught my eye. Someone was in our tutor room. At first, I assumed that it was the cleaner with his hoover and I briefly concerned myself with the safety of our fireworks and that of the cakes.

Having walked half-way across the huge area of tarmac in front of the building, I decided that I had a moral duty to return and check on the security of our crafts.

As I entered the room, Riley Boarer looked straight into my face. He was red faced and sweaty. This was the moment that the tyrant should be brought to heel.

It didn't occur to me once that Riley had been secretly practicing his dance for us all to enjoy. It didn't enter my head that Riley would be having additional reading lessons after school. I gave no thought to how this might end for either of us. I only thought of justice, defence, and protection for the others. He had been up to something and I was not going to tolerate this pig anymore.

Riley's head hit the desk. He hadn't expected any attack, so he went down quickly. His language hit me first, but I returned swiftly and screamed in English that I was going to rip off his skin. He lunged toward the door just catching the tray of cakes which then splattered, icing first, onto the floor. I felt the heat and then the rage as I grabbed at the back of his head and dragged him away from his escape route. He had taught me well. Block the door, keep shouting and drag tables for effect. He cowered at the back of the room and I jammed a chair under the door handle; no one was going to stop this revolution.

I took the glitter and glue, used by the girls, to step confidently and menacingly towards the little swine. Snot dribbled from his snout and spittle from his jowls. The glue and glitter spread over his head and down each cheek. A growl from the pits of my past crept up as my face loomed over this monster, "Let's see if we can make a silk purse out of you shall we piggy?"

The hammering on the door was the first distraction from the task ahead of me. The briefest moment to consider my actions. Could the bully learn a lesson? Should it be me who teaches him? Did I represent all of those tortured by this illiterate buffoon? Should I just rise above the actions of another and know that I was better? But of course, I was twelve, with no self-esteem and nothing to lose. This was my first taste of power and control.

I threw the bottle of glue and the pots of glitter at the door followed by a chair. Mr Cheval's face was at the window in the door and was calling out my name and asking me to open the door; first in English and then in French.

The first time my fist hit his pudgy little face, I was surprised just how much it hurt and wondered why he hit Sophie so often but remembering Sophie's torment, the blows rained down on him. The blood spurted from his nose as I stepped away to admire my handy work. He hadn't cried yet but for Muriel's sake he was going to. I dragged him by the front of his jumper towards the masks and pushed his face hard into one. It stuck at an angle into the glue and then I pushed him back onto the seat of a chair.

Morgan's plight crept into my mind's eye. I took his bag and emptied it onto the floor and took great delight in crushing the junior toys under my shoes. There was a reading book that I recognised from my early years of primary school so I picked it up and ripped each page out and into half yelling, "you can't read, you don't need books." It was tears I wanted for Muriel and tears I got. He begged me to stop, Mr Cheval called to me to stop, my head teacher ordered me to stop but I hadn't finished.

Riley saw a chance and dared to move. He wasn't scared enough and probably believed that he could still be the ruler. With management desperately trying to stop the situation, I knew that I had to up the dominance or I was lost, and no other odd little soul would ever have power again. He was an adolescent male and I was casting him out.

I reached for the fireworks. This was for Ben. Let's see how you feel when you can't breathe Boarer.

The hammering on the door became more urgent and was added to by Riley from the inside. I remember the look of disappointment and betrayal on Mr Cheval's face. The fireworks were made together because I could be trusted. But he had taught me that everyone has a social responsibility to stand up to evil and it would be rewarded.

I lit the first firework. After the first initial burst of sparks died down a plume of smoke belched out, so I lit the other seven in quick succession. The room filled with smoke, the alarms started screaming, and with great performance, the window at the back of the room was shattered inwards. The huge site manager stepped into the room and just calmly stated, "Out."

He had broken the spell and as he moved the chair from under the door handle the adults spilled in and swiftly dragged us both out.

The fire alarm screaming after 3:30 only brought adults out onto the tarmac. No one said a word to me. I knew that I would not see the year out, but Riley probably would.

(I must be odder than others.)

Chance 6: Liar

"I think that we can all agree that mainstream schooling has not been successful, so far, for John. We certainly cannot have him here whilst he awaits a decision on whether he is being charged with assault. It wouldn't be fair to his victim."

"Is it moral to exclude a child who is in care? I wonder whether we could offer an alternative option within our school."

"This is my school and we will be going into that meeting with a firm decision to exclude. If you don't think that you can fall in line, then don't come to the meeting. It will be my neck on the block if he kills someone next time; not yours!"

"Greetings to our excellent school. Will you all follow me to the meeting room? The Head will be along presently."

"Welcome everyone. I sent out a pack of the reports and, before we waste time, John will be permanently excluded from this school and the necessary paperwork is in the system already. This meeting must concern itself with the 'what next?' for John."

(Another immaculate suit.)

"We are looking at a more pastoral type of education for John. It does mean another move of home, but I am sure that he is used to that. The school being considered is attached to the home and therefore the staff can offer greater support with therapy and activities beyond education."

"What were John's predicted grades towards GCSEs?"

"He's academically very able but until he sorts himself out, socially, I am afraid it would be a fool who willingly predicts any outcome."

(My fault then.)

"We, the police, are currently considering a charge of physical harm, a lesser charge than physical assault. John has not been in any trouble before and has no criminal record. We will look towards some sort of reparation being undertaken but we have no decision yet. He does seem to have suffered some bullying here, but we can't advise on education matters."

I was seated between two adults that I had never met before, both of whom had smoked before this meeting, and the smell was clawing at my tongue. With smell put aside, they were both interesting to look at. The one on my right had extremely short hair and one arm covered in tattoos of animals; I liked the cat face. On my left was a huge lady with huge glasses. I don't know whether she was moving underneath her body mass, but she appeared to sit totally still. I had never noticed that all others moved constantly, even in tiny ways, until I sat next to her.

"We will send John's textbooks to his current home and his education will continue there until the local authority find somewhere for him. I simply cannot and won't have him here at 'my' school. We will communicate via email.

('My' headteacher no more.)

It took twenty-three weeks for a decision to be made for me. The notice came on the 15th of December that I would start my new education placement in the following January and so I had to move on the 19th of December to accommodate the staff holidays.

That was me, packed up and moving on again. I had got used to the pattern of moving but the dread of the new never left me. I rarely spoke so I did not tell anyone that I was sad to leave, after all, this was my most stable home; ever.

"Welcome, welcome, welcome. You have joined us just in time for Christmas. Fantastic, fantastic, fantastic. You are going to love it here. My word you've got tall. Let me take your bags for you. Come on. Follow me, follow me, follow me."

(The man, with the animal tattoos again!)

I followed this adult, who bounced as he walked, and I found it slightly habit forming. I began to bounce a little. He didn't stop chattering as he swung along, but I couldn't listen due to the physical surroundings being so different to any school I had ever been sent to. This was to be my school and my home.

"There are only twelve rooms, and this is yours. We respect each other's privacy and therefore no one will enter your room without your permission; no child nor adult. You must not go into anyone else's bedroom either with or without their permission. Let us chuck your bag in there."

He took hold of my black bin bag and flung it into the room without a second glance.

My first week was all about Christmas. I wasn't forced to join in with the decorating or shopping and chose to just observe. I didn't unpack my meagre belongings at all until January, but no pressure was ever applied to do so.

(Perhaps I eventually unpacked because no one insisted that I must.)

My fellow residents were seven in number, all boys, and all senior school aged. At first, they appeared to be confident and capable of adopting the swagger of modern youth. I thought that they had all had many Christmases here, but I was wrong. I thought that they would all be here during the Christmas school holidays, but I was mistaken, and I thought that I was the most anti-social but again, not so.

(I was starting to believe my own press.)

I was told that four of the others were going back to their foster homes for Christmas. Two of whom announced, over breakfast, that they would be seeing one or both of their birth parents, and that they would be receiving loads of money and piles of presents. Amongst these boys, the anxiety was high. They had swaggered a little more than the other residents, swore just a bit more often and deliberately hammered on closed doors but they were gone by the 23rd of December.

The absence of four, allowed me to observe three others more closely. I had chosen not to speak to them from the very start, but I was open to changing that situation if they turned out to be friendly.

On Christmas Eve, the whole household walked to the church in the local village; except for the lady who worked in the kitchen and a blonde boy who was going to help her.

(That kitchen always filled the home with comforts, warm and sweet.)

We sat through a service that told the story of the coming of our Lord. The church was decked out with flowers and candles; I thought it looked beautiful. We were told to be grateful and that God loved us all. On considering these words, I relaxed just enough to speak to the brown-haired boy next to me. Well, he could not have looked more alarmed and he began to whimper. The large adult who bounced when he walked, I now knew as Stan, lent sideways, and without taking his eyes off the preacher, whispered, "He's new like you and he doesn't speak either." I nodded as if to say that I understood and resorted to staring at the flickering candles.

(I wasn't the only new boy!)

Then out of the group silence and louder than the speaker, someone yelled. "Fat! Fat!" The tiny, blonde, female member of staff stood up and walked from the end of the pew holding the hand of the shouter and silently led him from the church. "Bastard Fat, Fat, Fat."

That left Stan, the mute boy, the huge lady, and me from the home to listen to the service. At the end we all trailed out and the adults shook the hand of the preacher and parroted, "God be with you, and merry Christmas."

My interest in the mute boy had been totally overshadowed by the shouting one. Once outside the church, my eyes searched for him. I would have never dared to say anything during such a formal situation, and I was slightly in awe of someone so brave. I didn't consider that it may have been involuntary.

On returning to the home, the cook had hot chocolate and marshmallows ready for us followed by toasted cheese sandwiches. The comfort that food brought was never to be forgotten and became my treat to myself as I grew.

On the morning of Christmas day, we were all given a personal gift and a mutual gift of a board game. The personal gift was that of a hoodie and trackies that matched. It was the standard choice of the social services and I got one every year.

(We all had different coloured ones of course. We weren't sheep.)

The game was Boggle. I love words and this game didn't require anyone to speak. Stan did his best to play the fool and lose.

My Christmas house mates were called Thomas, Morgan, and Connor. Morgan struggled to make eye contact with anyone and appeared to struggle with any form of words whereas Connor was happy to join in everything and offered as many obscenities as Boggle could offer; he was genuinely funny and made me laugh until my belly hurt. By the end of the day, I was even permitting Thomas to pat me on the back as I laughed at him hysterically laughing at himself. I learned that Connor had a form of Tourette's syndrome which just meant that he might, as far as I could tell, say whatever he thought without a filter.

Looking back, I enjoyed those few days together. No pressure, plenty of personal space, delicious food, and softly spoken adults.

January arrived as did the four others. Two Year 10's swaggered back through the door like streetwise professional teenagers. The tallest of whom ruffled my emerging curls and said, "Alright mate?" No answer required but I stood stunned and proud to be called mate. They swung their bags over their shoulders and lolloped off to their rooms.

(They were awesome.)

The dark-haired Year 9 arrived back in the evening heavily loaded with new stuff in boxes which he dropped in the hall. He headed straight for Stan's room and slammed the door behind him. When he did come back out, he was red eyed and downcast. The large lady, Sue, had gathered up his boxes and disappeared with them.

The other boy returned without fanfare or drama and it was only obvious that he had returned because he was at the breakfast table.

There weren't deep and meaningful discussions about the Christmases of the others but the Year 9 Harry shared that he did not see his birth parents as they had not turned up to the agreed meeting place, but Harry didn't think that the social worker had waited long enough. His foster parents had given him loads of gifts and money instead. Mark's birth mother had turned up but couldn't stay long as her other children were waiting in the car. I only know this because I overheard him telling Stan. He totally understood and she had promised that they could have a longer visit next time.

Harry cried at night. We could all hear him, but we knew not to make a fuss. He had to deal with it himself. Sarah, the little blonde would take him hot chocolate and sit with him, with his permission of course, until he went to sleep.

No adult inquired about Christmas events and the January school lessons started without drama.

All eight of us were taught together in the same room. The room was spacious, with a high ceiling and one huge window at the opposite end to the door. This room was very well equipped with computer technology, books of all genres and practical resources. You did not have to ask for a pen.

(Please Sir, Can I borrow a pen? Is always followed by, "Why haven't you got your own?" "You should be more organised!" Or worse still the sarcastic, "Didn't you think you'd need one today?*")*

Different staff arrived throughout the day to initiate the learning whilst the home staff took turns to become the class assistants. That support was incredibly appreciated, as they had started to become familiar adults and knew some personal histories, likes and strange traits.

The other young men, that is what the tutors called us, and we called them Sir or Miss, seemed to be comfortable with this system so it was easier to just follow their example.

I had anticipated being the most able in the room. I had always been so and therefore I had often been left to work alone unchallenged. That changed here. Jack and Jake, the year 10s, were much more able mathematicians and woke up something in me that I didn't know existed, competition. They were given textbooks to work from and they worked together. The maths Sir would offer these two whizzes a weekly challenge. If one of them could complete the *Times* newspaper maths teaser before he could, he bought us all a chocolate bar but if he won, they had to buy him one.

(That cost him dearly.)

I dreamed of being invited to join in one day.

(Yes. I was beginning to plan for a future me!)

Stan was always the member of staff we finished the day with, and he led a brief discussion time with us. Sometimes, just how the day had been, highlights and questions and other times the topic was driven by Stan. The first session was just a debrief of the day and ended with Jake and Jack rubbing the top of my head and calling me Curly as we left the classroom.

(My hair, for the first time ever, had been left to grow for a while and was indeed curly but a nickname was thrilling and from my first heroes too.)

Before dinner, we had half an hour to do what we wanted to, even if it just meant sitting quietly. Some of the others played games on the internet and others had a nap, Connor and I played Boggle as I knew he could match my word level and Morgan would go to his room. He still didn't speak but could read and write well.

Sarah, the tiny blonde lady, always popped her head in the door and checked on each one of us and with the briefest, "All OK?" she would be gone. I am not sure she ever stopped to hear the answer as I would never have said no.

(I really did not want to move again and wasn't ever going to be negative about anything.)

Within a month, I had seen that everyone of us 'young men' were talented in more than one academic area. I had been able to impress with my French speaking and knowledge of animal behaviours. For Connor, it was all about the words; his lexicon was vast. Jake and Jack, maths obviously and both were fast when they ran. Morgan read anything and everything and made complex notes about his reading. Thomas, the boy with Tourette's syndrome was an awesome artist and when he was drawing, he was totally absorbed in his effort and not a sound came out of him; except for the occasional fart but then we were teenage boys who were incredibly well fed here.

Harry and Mark, the Year 9s, seemed to me, to be excellent in every subject area. They were the best of friends and spent most of their spare time listening to music and crafting their hairstyles. They kept their distance but hadn't made me unwelcome.

I was proficient at signing and had begun, subtly, signing to Morgan. Just hello and goodbye at first, with the words out loud and then, over time, just mouthing the words. I progressed to please and thank you by our week eight of residence.

(Remember, we started at the same time.)

One Monday morning, following a weekend without the older boys, I watched Harry and Mark barge Morgan to the floor and kick his bag across the hallway. They were always like this on their return but generally settled down once Jack and Jake had had a word.

I lifted Morgan from the floor and collected his bag for him. He was incredibly light as was his bag; probably nothing in it, but it was his and we all had our ways. My remarkable reward for my kindness was a thank you sign from Morgan and I returned it with, OK.

OK was just the beginning. Morgan had reached out and I was happy to teach him more. This way he could communicate, when others weren't looking, and he was a quick learner. Stan had become aware of this relationship and on our way to lunch patted me on the back and thanked me.

During group time that day, Stan initiated a discussion about communication; both positive and negative, verbal, and non-verbal. This ended up with the year 9s sticking up their middle fingers and leaving. Stan congratulated them on making themselves clearly understood. When the session was over, Stan gave the rest of us the thumbs up.

Stan was clever enough not to mention sign language and instead came to find me in my room. He asked permission to enter, I agreed, and he sat on the end of my bed. I was seated on the blue armchair.

(We all had one.)

Stan told me about a chimpanzee called Washoe who had been a laboratory Chimp. Washoe was taught to sign 350 words but more incredibly, and to the surprise of her human teachers, went on to teach her baby to sign. He said that I had been kind and that would be rewarded with friendship. He added that I was becoming a fantastic member of his troupe and he bounced out saying, "See you at dinner Washoe."

Each evening, at 8pm, Sarah would walk along the corridor and gently announce that it was time to go to our own rooms and start to settle for the night. There was a routine to this that had become so predictable that it was comforting.

Jake and Jack, who had already showered and ensured their hair was perfect would call out, "Will do Sarah." Thomas would start with the word, "Tart or Slut and then apologise and finish with a "Yep."

From Morgan, nothing and from Connor an affirmative or indubitably. I was always already in my room so no reply was necessary, and she would just smile at me as she passed. But Mark and Harry, always begged for more time together and it was necessary for Sarah to go into the room to negotiate the briefest of extensions.

We ended our evenings with Sarah bringing hot chocolate and a digestive biscuit.

As Easter approached, I had settled quietly and obediently into life at the home. Routines were gently supported. Learning was challenging and exciting. The food that came out of Mrs Ambrose's kitchen continued to bring comfort and warmth. I had even started to fill out a bit and had noticed that I was becoming a young man, if you know what I mean.

As a troupe we could be hairy, sweaty, smelly, moody, and loud whilst also being clever, funny, quiet, and kind. There was a definite hierarchy and Stan was our alpha male.

As Easter approached, Jake and Jack began to make plans to Skype each other each day of the holidays and follow each other on Instagram; access to any social media was completely unavailable at the home. Thomas, Morgan, Connor, and I would be staying at home whilst Harry and Mark would be returning to their foster homes and were already telling us all about their parents visiting them.

Harry had grown more aggressive than Mark over the last week before Easter and Mark was almost following in his wake apologising for him but not daring not to join in. Within the troupe their relationship was the most interesting to observe.

I had been doing my own research into Washoe and then into other great apes and they would be considered the adolescents. Harry needed Mark so that he could enjoy a dominant position whilst Mark was becoming more submissive. We younger apes didn't even rate on their radar as important unless Stan was talking to us. That would cause a lot of arm waving and posturing. Harry's vocabulary, whilst always being aggressive, had become more sexualised and he was starting to encroach on Year 10 territory; they hadn't noticed yet though. He enjoyed walking behind them and swinging his arms trying to mimic their gait; it was quite sweet really.

On the last day of term, emotions were running high for those going out for two weeks. For the rest of us, it was just a case of staying out of the way. We watched each departure from the upstairs common room window.

Harry was picked up, according to him, by his paternal grandparents. They drove a large and nearly new Mercedes in what I would describe as Lego blue.

Jake stood on the drive with Jack waiting for their drivers. Jake had left his bags on the step and continually smoothed his 'High top fade' hairstyle with both hands taking care not to squash the top.

(I know this because I was trying to grow mine like Jake's.)

Jack had his sports bag over his shoulder and was nodding downwards and then lifting his head up making his long blonde hair sweep up and over. I don't know which one spent more time on his hair, but they were both impressive manes.

The taxis crunched over the gravel, doors were opened, and they were gone. Just Mark to go.

From somewhere downstairs came a screeching howl. It was difficult to tell whether someone was injured, or whether something had exploded in the kitchen. The first noise was followed by a short, more high-pitched noise and the sound of broken glass. I was still not sure that it was human.

Thomas started to whistle and hum loudly. Morgan ran from the room and I assumed it would be to flee to his own safe space. Connor and I stayed at the window and were the first to witness the stool from the office make a sudden appearance on the front lawn rapidly followed by a laptop.

Mark ran from the school building with his arms clutched around his chest. He flung himself onto the ground and started pounding the gravel and then tearing at his hair. It was obvious to us all that they weren't coming; whoever they were.

Sue, the larger lady of the staff team, waddled into the room and in a masterful manner, suggested that we make ourselves scarce whilst Mark dealt with his disappointment.

(She was The Management!)

We had seen Stan emerge from the building and stand on the step and Sarah sit down on the drive and begin to rub Mark's shoulders. They had this, and we were wise enough to follow Sue. Thomas dashed away trying, unsuccessfully, to stop the word 'Fuck!' from coming out of his mouth and headed for his own room.

Sarah did her usual rounds that evening and although I enjoyed the comfort of the hot chocolate there was a familiar anxious dread in the pit of my stomach. I had heard nothing of Mark and Sarah didn't offer any news, but I knew that he was still in the building.

(Our little troupe of four could become five. After all we were friendly and no threat.)

I could hear Sarah quietly cooing to Mark. She was able to be kind and brought comfort to all of us in her gentle way. Stan swung past my door and along the corridor. I heard him usher her out of Mark's room using a firm but quiet tone.

During the night, my sleep was broken by brief moments of panic. My breathing would become rapid and shallow until I was awake requiring deliberate control, counting and breathing in and out slowly until sleep took over again.

"Oi, Nigger."

Mark was injured and dangerous. Mark was angry. He was intent on making someone else feel worse and was looking to kick downwards and we were the downwards.

"Oi!"

On our trail down to breakfast, usually in silence, Mark's voice cut through the peace like a machete. He came at me low and caught me in my stomach. His shoulder crunched against my lowest rib and I collapsed to the floor. I knew to stay low and not challenge this level of spite.

Once I had been dealt with, Connor, Morgan, and Thomas were next to be taken down. Although he had come at me with his fists almost on the floor, he chose to stretch himself tall and wide. "Oi!" and it was much louder now, booming, low and menacing.

As Mark loomed up behind them, Connor turned to defend himself with his words, but he was just too slow. Each of Mark's large hands cupped both Thomas and Connor's small skulls and cracked them together. He stepped over the body heap yelling, "C U Next Tuesday."

(I still can't say that word aloud. I bury traumatic memories and I do endeavour to be polysyllabic.)

Morgan had the sense to fall with them and therefore be no threat to Mark.

Stan and Sarah appeared at opposite ends of the corridor. Stan allowed Mark to storm past him so that he could attend to us first. He effortlessly swept the other two boys into his arms and away to his office, with Morgan running behind him. Sarah helped me to my feet.

We walked quietly to the dining room where breakfast was set out around one table. There was no sign of Mark. She must have been aware of my fear and reassured me that Mark was now with Sue and would be staying there until a decision could be made about his presence in our home.

(Our home. That was comforting.)

She and I sat opposite each other and I sipped on my hot chocolate and she on her tea.

(She drank it black, no sugar.)

An ambulance pulled up outside the dining room window, and I looked straight at Sarah. According to her it was merely a precaution as the boys had head injuries and the staff here cared so much about us that we would all receive the same level of devotion.

By lunchtime, Thomas, Connor, Morgan, and I were all back around the table tucking into meat pies and mash potato; all homemade, and all steaming hot and smothered in butter. Sarah and Stan ate with us and we were discussing the merits of hiding Easter eggs inside over outside. It was as if this morning's events had not occurred. The physical evidence was still present, but the troupe had moved onwards.

Whilst we planned our next activities, a police car pulled up outside. Its tyres crunched into the gravel as it came to a stop. The driver's door opened and a large, exceptionally large, police officer extracted herself from the vehicle. Her passenger and fellow police officer remained in the car. There had been no lights, no sirens, and no drama to this arrival.

"Hi Sue."

Sue opened the back door of the car and ushered Mark onto the back seat. She continued to smile at him and ensured that his seatbelt was done up before firmly closing the door.

Strangely, she then hugged the police officer who then wiped a tear from Sue's face. Sue shrugged and walked away from the car and I presumed back into our home. The large police officer returned to the driver's seat and drove away.

No one ever said where Mark had been taken to, but the fact that he had gone, and we were told that he would not be back, allowed us to settle quickly back into the routines of our days.

During the Easter break Stan encouraged us to explore outside. The grounds that this home stood in were extensive and very rural. Stan taught us to make dens and challenged us to try and make them waterproof. He tested this by chucking a bucket of water over our handmade roofs, and we loved it. Morgan had become able to sign all his basic needs and confident enough to join in and had begun to giggle.

This was the first time I had ever felt tired at the end of a day and my soft bed and quiet room became a little haven at night.

During the last weekend of the holidays, I was aware that, as the youngest members of Stan's troupe, we were all becoming a little agitated. Thomas hummed, whistled, and cursed more than he had done in weeks. Morgan retreated to simple signs and stayed in his own room and even Connor was less sesquipedalian.

(He taught me that one.)

Our carers must have been very aware of this tension. The others would be returning to find out that Mark had left. There would be a change in the hierarchy.

To reassure us, Mark and Sarah began a new evening ritual; they read to us.

Sarah delivered the usual hot chocolate and accompanying digestive biscuit. But instead of tapping on the door, asking permission to come in and then leaving, she sat down on my blue chair.

"Would you like me to read to you? It will reassure you that we are all here for you in your home, and it might help you sleep."

I tried to explain to her that I did not enjoy fiction, but she insisted that I, just once, try listening to a historical novel. I wanted to please her as she had shown me kindness when others hadn't, so I agreed. She had chosen for me, *The Boy in the Striped Pyjamas*.

(Pyjama is Persian and was originally two words meaning leg and clothing. I love etymology.)

And so, a new routine began. Sarah only read a couple of passages for the first couple of nights and she read until I finished my bedtime snack.

The others returned without drama and Stan left discussing Mark's departure until we were all together having breakfast. He left out the violent details but explained to the older boys that no level of bullying would ever be tolerated here and would always result in a dismissal. He reiterated that his priority here was our safety and that nothing was more important to him. He finished the discussion by sharing that, in his opinion, we all must take responsibility for our own actions and that they are never the fault of others; we have choices.

The lessons began and the tutors came and went as was the rhythm of our days. The food was outstanding, and my company was friendly. The Year 10s, Jake and Jack, still referred to me as Curly and indeed my hair had become quite unruly; they were rapidly becoming hero-worshipped by me.

Harry was now our lone adolescent and needed to fill the gap left by Mark. He obviously didn't want to align himself with the babies, us, but was unsure how he could penetrate the close partnership of the older boys. They had such presence and implicit power.

Looking back, the first mistake I made was to encourage Jake to ruffle my hair. Harry had to break up this budding relationship so that there would be a void he could fill but instead of gently making himself invaluable to Jake, he decided to take me down.

Jake, despite having a magnificent afro, had very pale skin. He was immensely proud of his mixed heritage as it had gifted him with a handsome face which was going to be adored for the whole of his life.

(It might have become a curse, but I seriously doubt it.)

My hair had been kept short throughout my early years. I had it regularly explained to me that it is much easier to manage if it was treated to grade three on a regular basis. Here, in the words of Stan, we have choices and mine was to be like Jake.

As Sarah was coming to the end of her book that I had permitted her to read in my room each evening, she asked what I would like next. I suggested that she didn't read another fiction book in my room but asked if she could find out about how to tame my curls; just a little, I didn't want to lose my nickname. She assured me that she did not need to research that as she was the one who looked after Jake and Jack's hair.

(As a child, it is innate behaviour to be egocentric for survival reasons, but as we develop, we de-centre so that we might look after the survival of others. This generally means that as children we miss the small and subtle behaviours of others as we are busy growing and staying alive.)

But I have never seen Sarah attending to anyone's hair, I assumed that they did this grooming for themselves.

Sarah promised that we would begin the process of becoming more like Jake the very next day. She kept her word and taught me how to wash it first and discouraged me from washing it more than once a week or it would dry out and become frizzy, apparently not a good look.

Sarah made plans, that included me, to go into the local town on Saturday morning. I knew that she and the older boys generally went 'into town' on most Saturday mornings but I had never wanted to go nor was I invited.

Jack had asked for extra music tuition and his new tutor was coming the same Saturday and so there was space in the car. I had thought it was just going to be Jake and myself, but Stan had asked Jake to show Harry around the town as he was feeling left out. Jake being confident and kind, of course happily allowed another younger boy, as well as me, to tag along.

On reaching the town, Jake and Harry wandered off after agreeing a meeting time and place so that they didn't miss lunch back at home.

Sarah walked me through the unfamiliar streets. Sarah knew exactly where we were heading and took my hand and led me to a barber shop.

There were three chairs each with a person standing at the back of them and one other soul sitting within the chair. The chairs didn't look much different from the dentist chair. Some sort of pulp music was playing in the background; the sort that doesn't offend any generation, but none would choose to listen to. There were metallic noises competing against each other, and the music.

The man in the middle got up from the chair, took his coat, checked himself out in the mirror behind the desk at the door, smiled and left. It was such an automated and smooth departure, I guessed that this was his regular activity on a Saturday.

"Now young man, what are we doing for you this morning?" I really didn't want to speak but also didn't know what to say. Sarah jumped in for me and said that I would like my hair to begin to look like Jake's. This meant that Jake came here, and, this Miss might have been the artist that handled Jake's hair. I just added, "Yes please Miss."

She draped a black cloak over me and tied it at the nape of my neck. She patted, teased, pushed, and then said, "Let's get started then."

She asked me to sniff two different fragrances and give her my preference. I didn't recognise the first one and so chose the one that smelled like coconut. This she went on to spray onto my hair. Then I was clipped, combed, snipped at, trimmed, and stroked. It was not an unpleasant procedure, but I am not used to that much physical human contact. The reward for my frozen position in the chair for thirty minutes was a mini 'High Top Fade'; just like Jake's.

(I stood tall as we left through that magic door.)

Jake and Harry were exactly where and when they had agreed. Harry looked happier standing beside Jake as we approached; he even smiled at me or at least in my direction.

Jake was, 'well impressed' and referred to me as champ. I could cope without curly if I was now going to be a champion; I think.

(I needed to look it up when we got back to home as I didn't recognise this generational parlance.)

Harry knew there was a small opening between Jack and Jake on a Saturday morning, and he could not have me getting in there before him.

We hopped back into the car. Sarah and Jake up front and Harry and myself in the back with an empty seat between us. Jake turned the radio on and settled in. Sarah indicated and we left the car park.

"What do you look like monkey boy?"

That was Harry's opening gambit, but I wasn't to engage. Bullying wouldn't be tolerated here. We all have a choice. Obviously, he couldn't leave it there. He needed me to fear getting in that car with him. He stretched his arm across the back seat and whilst staring straight ahead, pinched my now exposed ears.

"You could be mistaken for a wingnut, Chimp."

When we reached home, I dashed for my room and hid behind a book. I knew that I had to let Harry have more Jake time or I was in danger again. However, Jack had finished his music lesson and was in Jake's room showing him the new riff he could play.

Harry went to his room and started throwing things around. Sarah went to calm him and eventually took him downstairs whilst stroking his hair and assuring him that she understood.

Over the next week, Harry could seek me out whenever we weren't in class and when no other person could hear him. Half-caste was his favourite. He obviously hadn't looked up the meaning of caste because he was using the wrong cultural reference, its delivery was meant to hurt though. He was implying that I didn't belong anywhere; no one would want me.

This was the one and only time I had been confident enough to consider my outward appearance and Harry was clever enough to know that it is where I would be weakest. Eventually, he began to deliver his venom in front of other members of the troupe. "John is your nose Roman?" Misunderstanding his question, I stupidly replied that I didn't know my heritage. Harry hadn't wanted an answer, he just wanted to state that my nose was roaming all over my face and begin to separate me from the troupe.

This continued at least once a day and wasn't showing any sign of stopping but here I could find sanctuary within my own room.

(Oddly, we all respected the 'no one in your room without your permission' rule.)

The daily routines continued, and lessons were excellent. Food was as comforting as ever, and I trusted the house staff.

Sarah had resisted her need to read to me but helped me with my hair routine each evening. She would sit in my blue armchair and read to herself. I think she knew I was upset as she would often stay longer and leave after I closed my eyes.

She and Stan still carried out their routines. One delivering hot chocolate and biscuits and the other meandering along asking, "All right?"

Harry never used the 'N' word, he was too smart for that but would take every opportunity to make comments about my appearance.

Eventually, I summoned up enough courage to ask Sarah if she could help. She asked me to tell her everything and I let it all flow out. By the time I had finished, I was in tears and starting to sob. She had moved from the blue armchair and sat on my bed alongside me.

"There, there," she cooed, "It's nothing but jealousy because you are so handsome, and Jake likes you."

"Settle yourself into bed and I will get you another cup of chocolate."

She returned with the warm drink and sat back into my blue armchair. She must have moved it closer to by bed as she was now able to pat my shoulder and it was a real comfort. She never required answers or eye contact, and this pleased me.

Stan could be heard coming along the corridor and Sarah whispered that she should be popping in on the others but would come back if I needed her. I thanked her for her kindness and assured her that I would be ok.

(I felt that she must be trustworthy because she went into every room and never shared what others had said or were going through.)

Sarah came into my room every evening after that. "Just checking that you are ok," She would coo. On the evenings that my hair required oil, she would spend time gently massaging each wave.

I had always been a lover of routine and this company became so regular that I hadn't observed any of the subtle changes.

Sarah stayed a little longer. She rubbed my whole arm and not just my shoulder. She told me how handsome I was and how I was just like Jake. She massaged my hair and neck. According to Mrs Ambrose, I was going through a growth spurt due to her excellent nourishment. This meant I was taller than Sarah and she had to reach up to oil the very tips of my curls. This meant that I could feel her body when she needed to get closer to reach. I did offer to sit down but she insisted that this is how she did Jake's hair and she wanted me to have the same as Jake; I had to agree. If I could be like Jake, then I would be set for life.

Harry had been taking pot shots at me all day. Jack and Jake were now including him in their school lessons, he was also taken out with them on Saturday mornings. Harry's hair had started to look good and I trusted that Sarah was making him feel special with a little one to one attention. Harry had managed to attach to the edge of the year 10 couple, but he needed to ensure that I was totally excluded. He had kept up the pressure and it was just too much. His new approach was to tell me about my birth parents and how much they must have hated having such an ugly, deformed brat.

(Of course, I knew that he could not know this as I knew nothing about my history, but it stung so deep and was my own personal agony; it still is.)

I went to bed early that night and buried my head in my pillow to prevent the sobs being heard. I could hear Sarah moving from room to room and would rather her not enter mine this evening, but I didn't stop her.

She cooed, she patted, she sat, she offered tissue, she rubbed but it made everything worse. My blue armchair was pressed up against my bed and Sarah sat so close. I could hear her breathing and smell the hot chocolate on her breath.

Her hand rubbed my arm and the familiarity of the movement stopped the sobbing, but I needed her to go and leave me alone. Slowly, her hand moved lower and slower. "There, there, beautiful boy." Her hand continued to rub my whole arm and then millimetre by millimetre across my tummy where she started to circle her fingers around my belly button.

I'd had wet dreams, I was a teenage boy, and they do, but I had never voluntarily ejaculated. It just happened. She stopped stroking me and handed me a tissue and as she left said, "You'll sleep well now my lovely. Just like Jake does. You are my other special boy."

I should have known that this utopia was too good to be true. Did Sarah comfort all the boys in the way she had comforted me? Did it matter that she did? Was I the only one? Was she the only one? These questions burned and I needed to gain access to that information. Would I get into trouble for just trying to find out?

(I'd got so many social situations wrong in the past and I wanted to be just like my hero.)

After the first 'event', I woke the following morning, with what I can only describe as, new sight. Sarah touched everyone and I'd never noticed before.

Morgan had her hand resting on his lower back as they walked together as if she was helping him along. With Thomas, she linked her little finger with his, but they never touched in class. Connor and she linked arms and marched to wherever they went. She swung her other arm to match his other one and they counted their steps together. Jake and Jack both had their hair teased. Jake, whilst standing, had his smoothed upwards. Sarah was tiny and had to be on tiptoe to do this and so her breasts touched his mid-drift. He clearly permitted this grooming and evidently enjoyed it as he had to sit down to hide the proof. She sat beside Jack and coiled his hair around her fingers whilst discussing his work with him.

I never witnessed her touch Harry in public, but they spent Saturday mornings together alone and his room was the last on the bedroom corridor. However, perhaps he was too aggressive for Sarah to comfort and someone else did it for him.

Her nightly visits always included her stroking me to sleep and I longed for her to stop. She didn't ask for permission to enter my room anymore so I couldn't refuse her admittance. I really didn't know how to handle this social situation and until I learned social rules, so I had been told, I wouldn't gain my GCSEs. I had everything to lose.

It was late into the summer term and Stan had invited Sue's police constable friend to come and talk to our troupe during our discussion time. Stan sat at the back of the room behind us. We sat in a semi-circle and Sue introduced her friend Pamela.

"Hi all, you can call me Pamela or Pam if you like. I work for your local authority and am a community liaison officer for your area. Stan has invited me to chair a question and answer session with you as you are all at a vulnerable age."

Harry started off with, "I'm not fucking vulnerable." He was all puffed up and sitting beside Jake. Jake hushed him and he sat back like a scolded puppy.

"Well, can anyone tell me the legal age of consent, in the UK, for sex?"

We all shrank back a bit as she said the sex word. Jack offered the answer of 16. Pam rewarded him with a thumbs up. The questions and answers flowed quite freely, mostly concerning stranger danger, drug trafficking, and sentencing until, out of the blue, Morgan spoke.

(Morgan spoke.)

"Does that mean that I can't say no until I am 16?" The question threw Pam for a moment. Stan had got up out of his seat and all eyes were on Morgan. His head dropped to his chest and he closed his eyes, so I decided to ask his question again on his behalf, mainly because I didn't know the answer.

"Consent? Does this mean we can say no?"

Pam shifted in her seat and strangely, became more police officer-like. Stan had moved forward so that he could see my face.

Pam's voice became sharper and slower as if she needed us all to clearly understand and remember this moment more than any other. "Consenting to have sexual contact or intercourse after you are 16 years old means that you have said yes, and you have a legal right to say no." She breathed deeply, allowing us to assimilate that piece of information and then began again but even slower this time. "In the UK. If you are under 16, you are protected by the full force of the law and no one, no one is permitted to have any sexual contact or sexual intercourse with you, at all." She left a slightly longer gap before presenting her final question. "Are you having sexual contact with anyone?" The question hung in the air like a blade. I looked at Jake. He slowly moved his head from side to side without taking his eyes from mine.

"Yes."

My lungs released their air, the weight of the entire atmosphere above me crushed down onto my shoulders and I fainted.

Sue said nothing as she ushered me into the back of Pamela's car.

(Telling the truth is a bad choice.)

Chance 7: Non-Conforming Unit

I sat on a grey plastic chair which stood on a bare concrete floor. The room didn't have a window but did have a toilet minus a seat or lid, some white toilet paper, and a narrow bed without any duvet or sheets.

Pamela had left the door open and I could hear her speaking to someone. She sounded cross. She kept walking backwards and forwards passed the doorway so she would enter my view and then disappear again.

"There is no other placement available at this short notice. It's the only room empty in the county right now. I know that, but I have no choice available to me. Do you have an alternative? He must sleep somewhere tonight and in one of my cells, on a Friday night, is not an option, believe me. He is fifteen and he will need support. I will ensure that you have all the information I have. Social services will be in touch immediately. He has not, I repeat, not broken the law this time."

Through the open, grey metal door, I watched Pamela put her phone back into her pocket and start to search through a pile of paperwork and eventually find the piece she wanted.

Pamela came into the room with me and sat on the bed. I feared talking to her but worse was the anticipated touch. She had removed her jacket and I wanted to ask questions about her belt but dare not.

Pamela explained that I would be interviewed but not tonight. She had arranged a room for me at a juvenile centre for a few nights and that there would be another move next week when a much better type of accommodation could be found for me.

(Juvenile centre and accommodation but not a home?)

I had no idea what to expect as I had never heard of a juvenile centre, but it was not going to be for long and then I would be issued a new home. That was my pattern so that is what I anticipated would happen.

A Landrover in police livery, pulled up outside the police station. Pamela tried to convince the driver to allow me to sit in the cab as I hadn't committed a crime, but the driver said that it was more than his job was worth, so I entered the back of the utility vehicle at the rear. In the back were two benches that faced each other. Pamela checked my seatbelt and then moved aside to allow the driver's assistant to sit opposite me.

We drove for what seemed like hours and it was impossible to tell what the outside world was like as the glass in the windows was thick and distorted the view. I stared at the floor for the entire journey. I didn't dare ask where we were going or what was going to happen to me. I had become so overwhelmed that forming the questions in my head wasn't an option. I felt that I was free falling and so utterly alone.

When we eventually stopped, I was ushered into a windowless reception, with eight strip lights on the ceiling, one of which had failed. The only contributions to décor was a murky, backlit fish tank, and a desperately sad pot plant. There was a handmade poster which carried a warning to all, that biting the staff would add an extra 28 days to their sentence.

(Sentence?)

The smell of fish and chips was mixed with the disinfectant stench that I associated with vomit. There was no smell of pencil and polish here.

The man who had travelled in the back with me, slapped a file of paperwork on the front desk and made it clear that he wasn't sticking around; it was late and that his shift ended half an hour ago.

I stood alone in front of the desk. Without making eye contact with me, the uniformed man behind the desk asked me for my name and date of birth. I gave him what I believed to be the correct answer. The uniform did not look up from the paperwork but made clicking noises with his tongue.

"You will be with us for the weekend and then your social worker will come and get you. Do you understand?"

I nodded because I understood each individual word. I couldn't comprehend where I was or what was going to happen to me.

A different uniformed person came onto the reception floor from a side door and asked me to follow him. I was taken into a side room where I was asked to remove my jumper. There were two adults in this room, one talking to me and the other utterly silent. I was then told to stand still while I was patted across my shoulders, along my arms and up and down my front and back. He then crouched down in front of me and patted down the inside and outside of my trousers.

(I couldn't have voluntarily moved.)

I was then offered my jumper back and told to sit on the BOSS. I stood rooted to the spot. I simply couldn't speak nor risk another error. I waited for a uniform with significantly more brass.

"The grey box over there. It's a scanner and it will show us whether there is anything inside you that shouldn't be." His hand waved in the general direction, but his eyes never met mine. My embarrassment spread like a flame from my very core and I was grateful for his disinterest.

(I still had some sense of personal dignity.)

Once I had been assessed, I was offered a hot drink. I didn't reply but a plastic cup was set down beside me with a warm brown liquid inside and I was instructed to sit down and wait.

The waiting room was quiet, and I was exhausted and sleep completely shut me down as if a plug had been pulled.

A soft voice was saying John and I jumped. A lady, in an identical uniform, except for the number on her shoulder, asked me to follow her. As I stood up, she handed me a folded tracksuit, a pair of white plimsolls and a transparent bag containing a pair of white pants. I followed her out of reception and another uniformed person stepped in behind me. I was driven down a corridor, through a door, across a courtyard and into another building.

"This is where you are going to sleep for a couple of nights. The other juveniles here are all on remand, waiting to go to court. Some are younger than you and some are older but not by much. You have a cell to yourself but that may have to change. No other juvenile may enter your cell unless we have put them there. All adults will ask to enter but they don't have to."

The room was almost identical to that at Pam's station, but the bed had a pillow and duvet and there was a TV on a desk. Two tiny bars of soap have been left out, two packets of toothpaste and a toothbrush plus a plastic hair comb. I could use those, but the close tooth comb wasn't going to be any use to my perfect hair.

(Still no toilet seat?)

As she turned to leave, she told me that the doors would be locked at 8:30. I had no idea that she meant the bedroom doors. I made the bed because that is what you should do. I cleaned my teeth and washed my face. With the door locked, no one could come in and make me do anything. I tapped my hair and got into bed. This was only going to be this way for two nights and might be the safest sleep I could get. I slept.

The following morning started with the sound of shouting. I was locked in and so could just listen. Most of the shouting was about being allowed out for breakfast.

When I heard the door click, I had expected an adult to step in, but nothing happened, so I just waited. Eventually I mustered up enough courage to peep outside the room.

"Oi! Why are you there? Breakfast now!"

Apparently, I was late for breakfast, but not knowing when, where or how to arrive at breakfast wasn't a defence so again I said nothing. The uniform 112 collected me and was not pleased that he had to 'babysit' me. He had better things to be doing, so he said. Breakfast was cereal and another hot drink; tea, I think. The crockery was plastic, the cutlery was plastic, the tables and chairs were plastic and bolted to the floor. Some others stared at me but not for long and then I was taken away again by the same moaning officer.

I was taken to an office on the other side of the courtyard. As I stepped on to the blue carpet, I immediately felt safer but not less nervous.

I had moved across the gap between two parallel worlds. Here was a coffee maker with coffee capsules in a variety of colours. All surfaces had been polished and I could smell the wax. A healthy yucca sat in a clay pot at the left-hand side of a huge wooden desk and, curled up against the radiator, was a dog. As my eyes smoothed the black fur, the tension in each muscle slacken and I could have peed, but I caught myself just in time.

"This is your interview. Everyone who comes here gets interviewed by me. Sit down and I will tell you how it is going to be and how you will conform.

(So not the, 'Tell me what happened to you,' Interview.)

I really don't need you around the other inmates all day. You will upset the routine and you are a safeguarding nightmare. We will complete this registration form together.

If my dog gets up to sniff you, will you stay calm? He is a petting dog. You may only touch my dog with my permission. It will help increase your oxytocin levels and therefore reduce your stress hormone. Hurting my dog will result in 28 days being added to your sentence.

(Again, sentence?)

I would have nodded but I was too scared to move. This uniformed lady spoke as if she was shooting bullets from her tongue. Although her register of language was intelligent, there was only one tone. She knew her script well and was just carrying out a necessary task.

I assured her, using a monotonal reflection, that I was exceptionally good with animals and that I recognised that her dog was a border collie who had an excellent intelligence and needed plenty of exercise.

"Back to the statutory paperwork please." She tapped her black biro on the paperwork. I knew that this form wasn't important to her as she had chosen to use black biro instead of the beautiful silver ink pen which stood in a holder at her right elbow. "I need to know if you have a drug or tobacco habit, and what is your usual alcohol consumption?" I just shook my head.

"You don't have an addiction, or you don't understand the question? "

"Sorry, no addiction," was my whispered answer.

"How do you feel about the first night?"

I shared that I slept all night.

"The youngest prisoners are housed in the (under school leaving age) USLA wing and you will continue to sleep there but will not engage in any of the activities. My officers will bring you to the reception wing before breakfast tomorrow and you will spend your day away from the other inmates. This will mean that you will not be going out into the yard either, but you shouldn't be here for long if you behave. I still don't have the details of how you ended up here but let us face it, no one gets through my gates without upsetting someone."

"What do you like doing?"

I looked down at the collie and answered that I am good at research and could do a project about dogs; specifically border collies.

I was smartly dismissed. The moaning officer took me back to the reception area where I sat down on a lightweight grey plastic chair at a, bolted to the disinfected floor, plastic table. A transparent plastic cup of water was set down in front of me.

(Reducing the use of plastic had not reached this far down the social ladder.)

On my arrival, I had noticed one poster but now I could see that there were many, all hand drawn and laminated. The suggestion was that they were reminding staff about the institution's values and listing items that must not be brought inside. Prohibited items included wax, chewing gum, magnets, plasticine, toy guns, mobile phones, Blu-Tack, metal cutlery, explosives, wire, newspapers, magazines, computer memory sticks, excessive personal medication, umbrellas. Things that will be carefully monitored include tools, yeast, cling film, rope, vinegar, glue, and tin foil. I doubted that the staff had made the posters, they suggested the work of youths, probably a task to ram home the messages and reminders of an extra 28 days.

I began to picture an officer putting on his uniform at home. Carefully checking himself out in a mirror to ensure the suitable air of authority had been achieved and then forgetting the rules and filling his pockets with explosives, a piece of string, a crayon and some cling film followed up by his loose change; Baden Powell would have been proud. Then walking into the reception area, reading the posters, slapping his forehead with his palm, and expressing he was such a silly Billy. He would have to hand that lot in and collect it at the end of his shift. This image grew a smile that lifted my cheeks a little.

After waiting patiently for thirty minutes. I could watch time pass by using the clock on the other side of the reception desk. I'd made mental notes of spelling errors in many of the posters. Tried to work out what crime could be committed using Blu-Tack and yeast, and arranged my research questions about border collies into biology, psychology, and sociology.

Eventually, I plucked up enough courage to approach the desk. There must have been someone watching a CCTV monitor as a tall uniform stepped out of a side room and asked if he could help.

I asked politely for paper, pencils, and books.

The door of the side room shut and minutes later the tall uniform pushed a trolley of books into the reception hall. He had balanced a pile of white paper and five pencils on top of the first shelf.

"These will have to do for now. I am giving you five pencils and when you have finished, I will be counting five back in. Any missing resources can result in 28 days being added to your sentence. Conform to the rules and routines and you'll be ok."

I nodded and wondered if he had counted the leaves of paper in the wad and I always tried to conform. The trolley of books was interesting just because the selection of subjects was so random. I like patterns and this bizarre library was a challenge to any order. There was not one text about any breed of dog, so not helpful as a border collie project but left alone I have always been able to occupy my own time.

I started to set the books out by subject, but there would have been too many subsections. Then I tried alphabetically by author, but the randomness of the sizes made the shelves messy. I considered ordering by colour and then resolved that size was probably more pleasing for others to look at. If I happened to be here long enough to read them, I would start with the tallest first and work my way down to the shortest. Having read every title, I resigned myself to reading them all in case there was one interesting fact in them, but I would avoid the one '*Where's Wally*'; I'd found him in year 6.

Having sorted the shelves on the trolley, I set to re-writing the wall posters. I thought that I could replicate the work of others but present the new versions with spelling corrections. I didn't think anyone would mind.

At just after 1pm, the door buzzer hummed, and the outer double doors slid open. A younger looking uniform waited between the two sets of doors until the outer doors slid shut and the inner ones opened. There was obviously not going to be an opportunity to slip out of reception without getting trapped between the doors.

(Where would I go anyway?)

As the officer walked across the reception floor the aroma of fish and chips wafted into every empty space pushing the disinfectant stench back to the floor. He carried a large paper bag in his right hand and swung his keys in his left. The doors on each side of the reception opened allowing the other uniforms to follow the youngster to the desk. The very tall officer popped up from behind the desk, I hadn't even realised that he was there, and waved the youngster towards him. With the bag handed over, the young uniform turned and smiled at me. I stared back at my latest effort on the table trying not to interrupt their lunch.

I purposely focussed on the shadings of a toy gun, desperately trying not to be noticed. I was tapped on the shoulder and a cardboard carton was placed on the right-hand side of my poster.

"That's for you. I hope you like fish. I trust you like chips. Would you like some tommy sauce?" I shook my head and mouthed thank you.

Inside the carton was a piece of steaming hot fish, a huge pile of fried potato chips and a wooden fork. I ate that meal as if I hadn't ever eaten before and left nothing. When I looked up, all the uniforms had left the reception to eat their lunches elsewhere. I felt that I might not conform to the inmate group behaviours, but I would try to conform to the uniform's wishes. This kindness would be rewarded with compliance.

(I made one addition to the poster which listed the banned items; wooden cutlery.)

At the end of the day, I was given a packet of sandwiches, a plastic cup of water and one of tea. I was taken back to my room, in the other world, where I washed, changed into the new tracksuit, and got into bed comfortable in the knowledge that I would be able to cope with one more day here.

This daily routine carried on, minus the interview, for five days and I was getting worried that I might be unwittingly becoming an inmate until I was told that I would be having another meeting with the boss: not the scanner.

Standing in front of the huge wooden desk waiting for the boss uniform to sit down, I wondered what it would be like to write with the beautiful silver pen. I eyed it, trying to imagine how it moved when being used.

"You can keep your eyes off that. Now. John. This morning, I had a phone call from your local authority, and they are arranging for you to attend a secure home and school. You will be picked up from here and should arrive there before it is dark. It is always scary when you arrive anywhere new in the dark and it is always worrying when you must leave here. Try not to get into any more trouble and I don't want to see you back. I have had two youths this year simply refuse to leave, but that was because they were homeless before they arrived and were surviving on the streets; one of whom lived in a bin. I understand that for some of you, this is a better quality of life than outside but off you must go. Count yourself lucky that they have found you somewhere to live. Thank you for the posters."

I had to sign out at the reception desk. I was told that I had to do so to meet fire regulations. I had arrived with nothing and I left with nothing. Standing between the two sets of sliding doors, I was a bit sad to go. It must be hard to leave if you had been here for years and it has become your family and your home.

"I think that we all agree, this is the last chance saloon for John. He could have stayed in Juvi and just cut out the drama in between, but no, the decision has been made to add him to our workload. We all know that there is very little we can change now."

"I don't know that we all agree. Can we just make sure that this is a positive experience for John? Every child is different."

"We consider him a young adult. He will be given his file in a couple of years and God knows how that will affect him. I gave up trying to read all the notes from previous schools. What a back catalogue!"

"Can I please remind everyone here that there has been a publicity blackout around John since the age of four? I don't know the details and only a very few know his birth name. Before John arrives, we must be sure we are all clear about the rules and expectations here."

"The expectations are, for John, as they are for all our YAs. Behave or you're out."

"If only someone had just given these boys a big hug occasionally perhaps, they would have felt loved and made better choices."

"That is a ridiculous idea and not helpful at all. If you were better qualified to do this job, then you would know that isn't love they needed, it was security! My God, I don't know why I bother."

Charlie was the driver. I knew that his name was Charlie as I had read his identity badge whilst it had dangled on the dashboard of the white people carrier. I had not noticed which make of people carrier it was, but they are all similar and I had lost interest in road vehicles.

He had chattered on throughout the journey of an hour and a half, without needing any input from me. Most of his monologue concerned himself and how he loved to run, where he had run to, why he ran, who he ran with and what his future running expeditions were to be.

(It always has amazed me how many people need to fill the silent void.)

I learned nothing about where we were going to and who I would be living with from Charlie.

My first sight of the secure home was two huge black gates. They opened as we drove towards them and Charlie shared that the car has a chip on board that gates recognise. He said that the gates weren't to keep anyone in but the other buggers out.

(I briefly pictured several folk clambering to get in with the intent of buggering someone but being thwarted by a shut gate and leaving.)

The image made me snort and Charlie mistook this sound as communication. The gates closed behind us with a resounding clang as they came together.

The buildings were a sprawling mess of wooden, one story, shacks. Charlie announced that we were here and before we got out of the vehicle, he noted the mileage on a spreadsheet. He bounded out of his side of the car and announced that this was my new chapter.

He then leapt at the large door and flashed his ID badge at a pad on the frame. The door swung open and he stood panting on the step waiting for me to join him.

"Tea? Biscuit?" I nodded and followed the happy chap through to a reception room. There were five, two-seater leather sofas arranged around a scratched, low-level table. A seat was suggested, and sit was the command. Charlie left and then smartly returned with a tray. The cups were plastic, the tea was brown and warm, the biscuits were stale, but nothing was yelling beware. The whole effect was that of an environment created by those who weren't trying too hard.

(I won't bore you with details of my bedroom or the routines, which were there, but not strict, more patterns than routines really.)

My meeting with the leader was brief and established that he was the boss. "If you choose to behave, you will be rewarded and if you choose to misbehave expect to be the recipient of sanctions. Your choice. No one is ever allowed into your room. No one is permitted to own a mobile phone. Phone calls can be made twice a week and only to permitted numbers using the landline in the office. Pocket money will continue to be paid into your bank account and, if you are rewarded with a trip out of here, you may make your own purchases. You are expected to complete the schoolwork set for you and to take part in some sort of physical activity each day, including Sundays. You will have a dedicated member of staff to whom you will address any problems you experience. Do you have any questions?"

I could not think of any questions because the idea that I had a bank account was dominating my every thought. I couldn't ever remember ever being told this or experiencing having any money of my own and it would take a whole month for me to write a note to my dedicated staff member asking for information.

Obviously, I completed every piece of schoolwork set for me and hungered for more. The teaching staff were happy to oblige with new textbooks and when the work wasn't marked, I marked it myself. I was, and had always been, capable inside the classroom, but the sport side of school had not been so successful. I had not found my niche but hadn't really looked for it either.

Charlie oversaw organising the sporting timetable. He offered team activities rather than formal, recognised games. Football was kicking a ball into the goal or passing the ball to one other person. Basketball was shooting baskets. Rugby and golf had been blended to become a bizarre careering around the grounds attempting to get a rugby ball into large potholes. Everyone had a ball and chaos ensued, but it was more fun than I had ever had 'doing sport'. There was also a gym, and Charlie encouraged us to use the rowing and running machines. He was fond of barking at us, "Fitness is the key to good mental health. Healthy body equals a healthy mind. Sport will save you!" I perceived that there was nothing to learn here but I was aware that I was getting faster and stronger within weeks of being here.

As the season was warming up, Charlie suggested a cross country run with a reward stop off at the local tea shop. We were required to add our names to the list on the wall board behind the leather sofa in the reception hall.

In this home, very few of the students spoke to each other. It was as if they knew this was the last chance kennel and they had to keep their heads down; don't get noticed. I did not get introduced to anyone but was able to identify everyone by sight before the end of my first month. I wanted to ask someone other than Charlie if it was safe to go out with these adults but instead, I just waited and watched who wrote their name on the list. Eventually, I added my own simple tag, John.

I wasn't even sure what a cross country run was. I knew that if we ran across the country from east to west, it was going to take us significantly longer than one Saturday but then again, I had been informed of Charlie's runs by Charlie and it was an outside possibility that he was capable of running for days.

It turned out that our first cross country run was a three mile yomp across the fields to the tea shop and back. I had estimated that a round trip of six miles should only take two hours to walk so a run should take much less, but I couldn't factor in how long the tea shop event might take.

Saturday morning arrived and I was nervous. The fear of the unknown kept crawling around under my skin, making me want to back out of the experience. We were all in our regulation shorts and T-shirts. I only had the plimsoles that I had been given by the Juvenile centre and I admired the multicoloured trainers worn by some of the others.

"Come on pack, we'll stick together for the first one, support each other and just see what we can do without losing anyone," barked Charlie.

An older, shorter member of staff joined us. She had a high-pitched yappy tone to her voice. She called out each name and it was the first time I had had to speak. Surprisingly, I did so without fear. I answered 'yes,' and she just continued through her list. She looked physically awkward in every way. She had the presence of a puppy who had spent too long in a kennel and was simply happy to be allowed out to play.

(Maybe fear is replaced by recklessness.)

Charlie called me to his side and patted his pocket. I have your card in my wallet and when we get to the shop, I will give it to you. He explained that I could only spend forty-five pounds on any one transaction with each swipe. I was too embarrassed to ask what this meant but planned to watch what the others did.

"You have five hundred and forty-five pounds but without a four-digit code, you can't access the whole amount in one go. When we go into a larger town on a reward trip, you can go into the bank and request a new code to be sent to you, but forty-five pounds will be more than enough for today's trip."

I could not imagine how I had accrued such a large amount of money, but I was excited. New trainers would be my first purchase and I couldn't wait.

(I had not been excited since primary school and that involved a bee.)

That first Saturday morning was successful. We chased each other just as we did when playing rugby golf. I hadn't any concept of what three miles would feel like, but I loved the feeling of being breathless, hot lungs, throbbing heart. It felt like being free, flying, chasing, I, for moments, was my best self ever.

I learned to swipe my card in return for a hot chocolate and a slice of Victoria sponge. We ran back in a race style with Charlie leading the pack. I felt like I belonged.

(A first.)

As a reward for a successful event, I was invited to go shopping. One of the others and I were asked to take a list of provisions for that evening's dinner and to choose a dessert for everyone. This felt like a lot of pressure and I wanted nothing to go wrong. Charlie, sensing my nervousness, reassured me that at no point would we be left alone to make an error.

"Losing one of you would put me on the front of *The Sun* newspaper on a no news day and I am not up for that John. I'll have my fifteen minutes of fame when I successfully run up a mountain for charity, thank you."

As it was Saturday, Charlie said that it had been his intention to go to the bank with me but he had got caught up with a trivial event at the home and we were too late for that but we would have time to go to a sports shop and look for trainers before we bought food.

Events that didn't include me held no interest anymore. I didn't want friends, I didn't trust adults, and I knew that no home was permanent, so I focussed only on myself. I was also grateful that Charlie didn't share the trivia.

Getting to the town was easy, white people carrier, two young adults and three staff. We stayed together and hit the sports shop first. Walls and walls of training shoes was the first hit. Charlie was in his element. First, the sizing had to be done. Then, in my bare feet, I was asked to run on a treadmill. We then watched the images and Charlie confidently showed me how I was running and how the right trainers would help me improve my gait and therefore become faster and endure for longer. He seemed to pant with exhaustion by the time we left the shop with a cross training Adidas shoe in urban lilac, costing less than £45.00 so that I could swipe my card for them.

I was unbelievably proud of my new shoes. My first. Paid for with my own money. My choice. Charlie gave my shoulders a hug but then openly checked himself and apologised for touching me. I hadn't even noticed. My trainers were in my box, wrapped in my tissue paper, all being carried in my paper carrier bag by me.

(No plastic at this level.)

The supermarket offered no interest or irritation. Nothing penetrated the sensation of holding the string handles of my bag. The other young adult chose the dessert, trifle, and the staff quickly nipped about picking up the other items for dinner. I think it was supposed to be a lesson about budgeting but even school staff have got better things to do on a Saturday. All I wanted to do was get back and try my new shoes on again. I was so proud.

I made a personal decision not to ever spend more than £45.00 on anything and kept a balance of my outgoings in my head. My needs were few and I spent little.

We continued to enjoy cross country running each Saturday. Charlie had put together the fastest of us as a team and we would sprint short distances, within the grounds, each Wednesday afternoon. He also introduced the morning mile and so I was able to hone my newly discovered skill. I was a runner. I didn't worry about who was quicker or slower than me, I just loved the sensation it gave me. The feeling of reaching a peak and then kicking up a gear and pushing harder as the endorphins picked up was exhilarating. When running as a group, I was always really running against me.

The first four months of being at the secure home school were a blur. I hadn't paid any attention to time passing as I assumed that I would have to leave after some incident. I tried not to have incidents but as I had never been able to predict what these incidents would be, I knew that I couldn't avoid them. I did as I was asked when I was asked. I followed the rules and routines.

I had decided that I preferred summer this year as it provided me with the greatest number of daylight hours. This meant that I could run every day, at least twice. Charlie designed running plans, and set aside time for me, and others, to use the gym to strengthen our core muscles; he had become quite the trainer. He was very keen on us becoming agile as well as fast. We were a small group of misfit adolescents, but our sport kept us busy, so I hope that we didn't offend anyone during those fine times.

At the beginning of July, a notice appeared on the notice board, attached was a big arrow which read, 'please read.' It announced that there could be an opportunity to take part in running trials and that more information would be forthcoming. It required us to sign up if we 'might' be interested. It would be considered a reward so that anyone on sanctions would not be eligible.

The event was to be on the 23rd of July, a date I had never reached in the school calendar. Charlie had become the official trainer of his own running kennels. Four of us trained with him every day. He ensured that we consumed the correct food in the required amounts for maximum effect. He even had us running in the shallow end of the local swimming pool as resistance training! Charlie continually barked at us, telling us what he was doing so that we might be chosen and become winners.

(Maybe he could see his own escape.)

He kept us busy and as a result I had become leaner and stronger than I had ever been before. I kept my hair as Jake had done and declined the offer of a crew cut to gain 'maximum streamlining'.

(Going too far Charlie.)

The Saturday before the main event, Charlie announced that our usual cross-country run would not be across fields but on sand. Good resistance training and fewer opportunities for any of us to get injured.

The four of us and six staff piled into two people carriers, both white, I have no idea where the other one came from; perhaps we had always had two. It was those details that I had stopped being interested in or even noticing. Three staff and two young adults in each.

I was seated next to Charlie and he, as I knew he could, talked the entire journey. He barked on about muscle strength, mental health, visualisation, myoglobin, and DNA whilst paying no attention to his fellow passengers.

I was excited about being on a beach as I had no memory of ever having been on one. I had only ever seen them in books or on the TV; usually a David Attenborough programme. I was excited because we were going to run, and I was excited that I was being rewarded for getting things right. So, I looked across at the other young adult in the car and nodded at Charlie and rolled my eyes in a moment of trail comradeship. He, obviously having listened to Charlie, felt the need to explain what Charlie was saying. He clearly, and without taking his eyes off my face, explained that whilst he could be considered a pedigree, I was more mongrel which could offer benefits if you take into consideration my mixed DNA. Which, in his opinion, was usually a disadvantage but when running was the event, I might indeed have an advantage. "All the fastest are black."

I sat stunned. Charlie hadn't heard as he was still yapping on about 'how to be the best runner' and the two adults were engrossed in their conversation and hadn't paid any attention. In silence, I allowed this information to permeate through all my understanding of biology and history.

We arrived at the beach car park and disembarked. There was a brief discussion between the five of the adults about whose turn it was to get the coffee and how long they should buy a parking ticket for. We stood still in a small group in unfamiliar surroundings. Charlie bounded over to a low wall of huge rocks, put his hand to his forehead as if he were on a ship's bridge and then whistled us over.

"Right guys, we have four hours until the tide turns. We can run as a group to warm up and for you to see the natural boundaries of the beach. I will continue to run on the beach so I will be around if you need me. The other staff will remain on this wall with the first aid kit and your water bottles. You may return to them at any point and rest. This will be our last opportunity to run off site before the trials so make it count. "

Charlie led us out onto the wet sand towards the waters' edge to begin the warm-up. We ran together and I avoided the waters' edge to prevent my trainers from getting wet. We ran back on the sand at the top of the beach, just below the cliff base. My legs wobbled on the unfamiliar shifting dry sand, but I gained the thigh burn quicker than on any hard ground and I loved it.

As we ran, Charlie weaved between us, giving each of us personal tips.

"Visualise the ties that hold you to the ground being released. Let yourself fly. Discard your earthly tethers, shake off the chains that bind you."

On our return to the car park he congratulated us for achieving this standard of sporting opportunity. He stated that although we were all different, we could all be the same when running. I didn't even look up.

We were given permission to run as we chose to and told to make it count. Charlie ran off onto the beach on his own mission to become something or someone else.

I knew that I could run far without fatigue, but I had never tried long distances at speed. If this was going to be the only opportunity, I had to test myself now. Charlie had said that the beach was two miles long, so four miles round trip.

Two others were marking out a one hundred metre track along the water's edge which was perhaps their best discipline. The other was trying to keep up with Charlie.

(So needy.)

I didn't concern myself about the trials but was incredibly grateful for the running expedition. I walked to the top edge of the wet sand. Here it had dried out enough not to wet my prized trainers but hadn't become so dry that it would shift about. I gaged it to be the perfect fit for my type of running. As Charlie was in the distance, I risked tying my hoodie around my waist. He wouldn't approve of this wind resistant choice but if was my only other possession with me today and I chose not to leave it behind in case someone took it.

I had considered starting with a slow jog and building up to a good pace but as one of the sprinters whizzed past, I just couldn't stop myself. Out of the gates and go.

The air was fresh and full of encouragement. The rush of the sea coming in and out filled my head. As I sped up the salted wind pushed against my face. I was in the zone and I was fast. "Detach from the anchor that holds you!" I pounded the sand, knowing that the footprints I left behind would be washed away. The opinions of others meant nothing. I was free.

My legs burned, my lungs were on fire, and my heart beat faster than ever before. Just when I thought that I could go on no longer the wind, it or I had changed direction, caught my back, and pushed me onwards.

The air became chilled and I reached for my hoodie and I pulled it over my head. I was running up a slope now and became aware that the ground under my feet was harder than the sand had been. The light had changed. When I turned around and looked back to consider my run, I looked back at a beach far beneath me. In the distance, I could just make out the others still running back and forth.

I could have turned back and joined them, but I chose not to. I ran, I ran forward to my own destination and it excited me. With no fear, and nothing to lose or anything precious behind me. Whatever I was, I had reached maturity and could make my own good choices. I could survive because I was not held back by anyone or anything. With the sun on my back, my bank card in my pocket, my urban lilacs on my feet, I was free, free to migrate. I am someone who moves.

Chance 8: NEET

"He has been reported as a missing person. He will be sixteen in six weeks and then we must consider that he has the right to choose his own path unless there is any evidence of wrongdoing."

"With all due respect, he is still a child and a child in care; a child looked after. Surely, he should be considered more than just a missing person. Who is taking responsibility for his care? This is all very messy. He will be another statistic; not in education, employment or training."

"He didn't go missing on my watch, so I am not taking the blame. His picture has been circulated across all agencies, but it is not a recent one due to his continual movement and his publicity blackout status, very few photos have ever been taken."

"We did all the necessary risk assessments required to take him to the beach. He ran away. We could not have assessed for that. Our staff have been traumatised by this event. One is now on long-term sick leave and the other two who accompanied him on the trip out, won't leave the building with any child. He has spoilt everything for everyone else."

"Can I bring everyone back to the reason we are here? What is to be done next? We must all ensure that every piece of paperwork has been checked, double checked, and please, please ensure that each piece is signed and dated. We could all end up in court if this turns out to have a tragic end."

"There has been activity on the bank account. There was activity on his bank account last week, so we know when and where his card was, and that food was purchased. Currently, we don't have the manpower to investigate further but we believe that John is able to access money and assume that he has food and somewhere to sleep. It is still early days and he may just walk back through the gates."

"I doubt that very much and he wouldn't be permitted to stay if he did."

"Is John considered a risk to others or himself?"

"Let us say yes to be covered. We will meet again in one month and assess the situation. Will you still be his social worker?"

"Probably not as I was only temporary anyway. He would be due a change of staff at sixteen, but I expect someone will attend the meeting."

"School staff won't be at the next meeting as it falls during the holidays, but someone will make the next one when the school year starts again."

"Let's all agree to keep these meetings formal, tight and professional. No one is to blame. John has made a choice. Let us hope that he is safe. He is a ward of court and therefore we must hope to find him before he becomes another damning statistic."

For the first few weeks running was preferred. I could easily sleep at night as I was always exhausted. I bought food when I was hungry and washed whenever I came across a public convenience but as summer days became shorter, it was obvious to me that I needed to find something more permanent, dryer and warmer. I had tried living in the town but had been beaten up, pissed on, spat at, and so cold. Dogs on leads had been allowed to crap on my clothes and they looked down their furry noses at me, but I am not a dog, so I never reacted. There is no shelter from the worst of humanity on the streets. I asked nothing of anyone and took nothing, but I was not contributing either.

I chanced upon my home, my hobbit house if you like, whilst enjoying a few days camping in a wood. I moved in when the diggers clanked their way over the turf and lorries piled up the materials needed to build homes. Serendipity, I profited by being in the right place at the right time. I had found my home and I could begin to provide and learn again.

The building posse are recognisable and differentiated by their hard-shell hats. Grey hats are for visitors to our neighbourhood habitat. The boss wears a white one. He's an enormous man both in height and girth. Most of the general workers wear yellow. The safety inspector wears a green one and everyone wears the correct one when she turns up. Blue is for the electricians or carpentry crafts who fly in occasionally, do their bit, and leave. Orange shells are those who lift heavy loads or marshal the transport access. Brown is worn by those who concern themselves with heat and, finally, the pink ones; lose or forget your hard shell and you'll wear the pink one. Everyone usually has a yellow jacket to go with their shell so that they are easily seen contrasting with the environment but occasionally an orange one arrives usually supporting a brown hat, roadies. I am told that these orange jackets can also be seen on the railways of this country but I have never been on a train and am unlikely to have that experience in my current circumstances but who knows what my future years may hold.

Stacey is a yellow coated yellow hat. He has become my friend. He is only a couple of years older than me and rides a black shiny scooter. Stacey keeps away from the general workers and other trades because he takes his orders from the alfa white. He doesn't have a skill, but he keeps the site tidy, fetches, and carries materials for all his co-workers and so makes our housing estate safe. He struts around the site, whistling, clicking his fingers and even sometimes dancing to the amusement of everyone except the boss. When he approaches the boss, it is from the side with his head and shoulders sloped downwards until his dominant protector speaks to him. Once the relationship is reaffirmed, Stacey quickly returns to his fun and chattery self. Stacey is restricted to lighting his burn stack to Friday afternoons otherwise he'd have one each day; he loves lighting fires.

When Stacey isn't too busy, I am permitted to help him tidy up the site to keep everyone safe but only if I wear my yellow hat. I help others on the site and in return I have been given a high viz jacket so that I too am safe.

In return, I am treated with respect and kindness. I want to be like Stacey.

The boss appreciates my help in taking his sandwiches each day. His wife always packs the same ones and he prefers the meat pies from the van that turns up at eleven each morning. I imagine that he thanks his good lady every day for his delicious lunch; I know we do.

If I was a deity and spent any time watching the activities of these characters beetling about, moving aggregates from one place on the planet to another, creating temporary structures and then taking them back down again. Digging large holes and then filling them back in with different materials. I would marvel at the pointlessness of their existence. Then again, if there are deities, they probably have better things to do than sit and watch us little people.

Last Chance: HOPE

The hard hats have left the estate for two weeks, but they will be back soon. For the next few days, the hours of light will become fewer, but I, along with my family eagerly await the change.

For now, even the hardiest of us are reluctant to be out in the evening. I go out once a week, usually with Charlie and Jake to collect our £15.00 and gather our provisions for the week. Recently, we have purchased a can opener as the bargain tins often do not have a ring pull; we do like a bargain. Cans are our best way of keeping a good larder. We cannot have hot food because Stacey isn't going to light a big fire for the next three Fridays, but I am planning a surprise for the 25th and will cook a Christmas steak. I have a small stash of dry pallet wood and two bricks. What a treat?

Stacey and the boss are the only two who visit our home, but the others always call out if they have something I can use; before Stacey burns it. I am part of the gang and I feel accepted, but I am the only one of my family allowed onto the building site.

My family moved in during the autumn months. I had kept up my running practice and quite by chance ran into Charlie. He was bounding along a ridge of the Downs heading west and I was, head down, sprinting up the same ridge heading east; we literally ran into each other. I invited him to share a sandwich and from then on, we were running buddies.

Jake, we met in the town. He was strutting through the market with the arrogant air that only an adolescent can have. We dashed to catch up with him and I tapped him on the shoulder. He almost took my head off with one almighty swing but was swift enough to cancel the motion as he realised that it was me. We went through the usual tapping of hand ritual and then caught up. He said that he was living in assisted lodgings but hated the rules. He said that when the owners of the lodge threw shit at him, he really threw shit back, so he had to stay out during the day. We, of course, gladly offered refuge to my hero. That great ape was so funny, and his confidence was contagious.

Miley snuck in during one rainy night and just stayed but none of us minded as she was so sweet and could warm the coldest room with that smile of hers.

Warren arrived injured so we stuck him back together and supported him until he was well enough to go, but he had missed the mass move that his other family does each autumn, so he asked to stay for the winter.

Riley, I found on the site, rooting through the bins after the site had closed. I felt sorry for him but knew that he could make life very difficult for the rest of us if he were allowed to roam free so we agreed that he could stay on the condition that he always stayed in the woods and never went beyond that boundary. He agreed on the condition that he did not have to work, and we would always share our food with him. In return he said that he could keep the garden tidy and scrap free.

Jane bumbled in as the nights grew colder. She asked to stay until next spring but assured us that she needed nothing beyond sleep and to keep dry and would be no bother. She brought with her harmonious song and she liked to buzz about dusting when everyone else was out. Her sting proved helpful to keep Riley inline more than once.

(That boy takes his time to learn.)

We all established our routines and by the end of November we were settled. Respect, responsibilities, and rights were upheld and by our shared social abandonment we came together as a family.

Some people might consider our lifestyle choice to be chaotic, but we have a home and it is dry, warm, and clean; and happy. We are not homeless. We try to help, when we can, those souls who do not have our luxury and sleep in wet sleeping bags with pieces of cardboard as protection from the freezing ground temperature in shop doorways. We leave cans of tinned fruit and soup when we have spare, always with the ring pull tops; we have the luxury of a can opener, but I doubt that some of those ladies and gents do.

I am fascinated by the human condition and now am forced to learn by observation only. I could use the public library, but the reference books are often out of date so for the present I enjoy watching and reading newspapers; there is a range available in the site canteen cabin. I have noted that the term homeless is not preferred as rough sleeper is more palatable. It suggests that these folks have chosen some sort of extreme camping for fun or fashion.

The local department store had begun to prepare a Christmas display during November. We didn't keep note of the time or the date as they meant very little to us. It must have been November though because the display was an enormous advent calendar. This would work well for them as directly opposite the store was the cathedral. It offered those who regularly go to the services a connection to the store and those who only attended the services during advent would pass by on their way to salvation and would probably pop into the store afterwards.

Both city establishments must have despaired of the small community of 'rough sleepers' who had to be stepped over to get to their chosen destinations. We all agreed that we would have liked to all rush into the Cathedral with its lights, trees, warmth and glitter and scream, "What would Jesus say?" but we were far too scared.

Our nearest neighbours were Mr and Mrs Colin and Julia Draper, and they have bought their dream house in the country. Their plan is to raise a family in the fresh air. Selling their flat in central London, they were able to buy their house without a mortgage. We know this because a letter addressed to them was taken to the site office by mistake so the boss asked me if I would deliver the letter to them. I was dressed in my high viz jacket and my compulsory hard hat and gladly accepted the request. On reaching the door, and to be more neighbourly, I knocked on the door instead of just pushing the letter through the letter box.

I think that Julia might have been feeling starved of company because, although she did not ask me in, she did feel it necessary to fill me in on her entire history and reasons for being wealthy. Apparently, nothing could spoil this move to the countryside. She was relieved that they have moved away from the beggars, rough sleepers, disruptive protesters, and dirt. They have five years of married city life behind them and this is the next step in the plan to the perfect life together.

(How was I going to tell her?)

Julia babbled on about how happy they were with the chaffinches, blackbirds, and robins in their garden, and delighted with Mr Squirrel who raids her bird table. She then took her post and thanked me.

I had met the neighbours and felt included again.

We could see Julia watching her wildlife from our home and always gave her a wave if we were out and about, but I do not think that she could ever see us as she did not ever return the wave.

· · ·

Julia had risen late, and the day had begun around her sleeping self. Colin always left the lights on and then had the audacity to moan about the electric bills. He had not quite got used to the fact that running a large home would cost more than a flat, but he would. She hoped that the tradesmen didn't come to her door again today. The postman really did need to get his act together after all her house was the biggest on the estate and was clearly marked. She felt surrounded by people who couldn't organise themselves and had to place her at the centre of their own ineptitude. She really didn't have time or energy to sort other people out nor did she want to listen to their needs or wants. Colin should learn to turn the light out if he is that bothered. She made herself a fruit tea and gazed out with pride at her beautiful chosen environment.

She was in her maternal element. First trimester nearly over, the books shared with her what to expect next. Her brand-new carpets were soft underfoot and the nursery was just like the one she'd seen in Hello, gender neutral of course. She was considering a new car. The smart car was a city car, but the countryside required something bigger as did the new pushchair which now proudly stood in her wide entrance hall.

Standing behind her bi-folding doors Julia observed her first garden. It was neatly bordered with a six-foot wooden fence and Julia stared at it wondering which fruit she should grow up it. Her child would be able to pick fresh organic fruit whilst playing on the lawn.

She eagerly anticipates the arrival of all her city friends who are coming to stay for Christmas. Wait until they see how brilliantly she is doing. Everything must be perfect.

. . .

Charlie wakes at sunrise and tiptoes over the sleeping family and meets me outside. His black and white fur coat flattens as it rubs off the light cover of dew against my leg. Miley is awake and is quietly going through her morning cleansing routine; always face first, then she works downwards until she finishes off with making sure the skin between her toes is moisturised to her liking. I am always the first one to leave our home. I am the tallest and so, due to the height of our ceilings, I require a huge stretch. The sky is clear and bright blue, but I am guessing that there was plenty of cloud cover during the night as none of us complained of being cold and I hadn't noticed Jake move over to wrap his arms around Riley. It was good that they got on as it was those two souls who could really create disharmony in the ranks.

I know that it is the 23rd of December thanks to the advent calendar in the window display. We try to go and see what was behind the doors on dry evenings. The window remains lit up and has a faux fireplace with stockings and models of reindeer and penguins on fake snow. It looks lovely and there is a new product behind each door. It does look inviting, but I do wish that they would not promote the idea that penguins live with reindeer. I like the colours and the ideals, but I find it difficult to understand the social protocol, etiquette, or customs of the season.

(But then again, I do not understand why anyone would use a disabled toilet, it has been disabled, or what a crime support unit is, surely a victim support unit or crime prevention unit. Neither can I begin to guess what flexible storage systems are, bubbles perhaps. And this year, 'Traditional Christmas' turkeys are being advertised in the butcher's shop window. What the fuck is an untraditional Christmas turkey? A turkey.)

We, for the first time ever, look forward to our Christmas and to being suitably consumptive as we would not like to leave society all together and it is our plan to contribute more significantly when I turn eighteen; adult.

We have, like most people, planned our day. First a walk into town to answer the question of 'What's in number 25?"

After our walk, we intend to all have a meal together and then snuggle down and listen to the environment around us. With the site team away, there is a real beauty in the silence when the machines have been turned off.

I will prepare a tin of pears for breakfast; 15p in the bargain basket. It is easier to take the can outside to open it as it prevents spillage and the others don't argue about who's turn it is to use the tin opener, but we'll eat together inside. Today is the day to start gathering dry grass and wood ready to heat our bricks for Christmas day.

. . .

"Police please. There is a man with a gun hiding in my woods."

"Mrs Julia Draper. Number one Heather Moor Drive."

"Hello. Yes. There is a man in the woods behind my house with a gun. He is waving it about. I am a heavily pregnant woman on my own and he is going to shoot me! Definitely a gun."

"I have locked the doors. I can see him very clearly."

"My friend in the metropolitan police said that I must tell you immediately that he does' have a gun'. Of course, I could be mistaken but I am telling you, it is a gun. No, I do not know which type. Does it matter? It looks like a handgun. Please come quickly."

. . .

The sirens pierced the peace and the moving intermittent blue flashes moved through the roads just beyond the building site. We watched and all hoped that nobody had been hurt. We have waved at Julia this morning, so we know that she is OK and doesn't need our help at all.

The flashing and noise stopped as quickly as it started, and we went back to our breakfast chatter.

It was Charlie who first sensed something and laid flat against our floor. Riley, seeing that Charlie was worried, moved to the back of the room.

Jane suggested that she take a sneaky look outside as she was the smallest and no one ever takes any notice of her anyway. She was still winter wobbly, but she made her way out into the daylight. She spread out her arms and without a second glance was gone.

(No loyalty!)

Warren stayed stuck to the spot under the table. Charlie and Miley joined me just inside the doorway. We were being nosey and trying to catch a glimpse of what was happening.

. . .

AFO Veronica Edwards was bursting with enthusiasm. She'd chosen to join her local police force after leaving college. Her careers officer had stated that she would be excellent in the role and advised her that, as a woman, she might have many opportunities offered to her beyond that of her male constables.

"Given the percentages and recruitment drives needing to meet diversity quotas and all that."

Veronica had never cared much about promotion, opportunities, or career. If she had not got a job, her parents were going to insist on university, so this suited everyone, and the pay had sounded good.

Although Veronica had drifted into the career, she excelled. She found that she really enjoyed working for the public, the job kept her fit and the social life was interesting. After her initial training, she had spent two years as a probationer in a city near her parent's home, so she had continued to live with them.

After that she had been selected to work within the counter terrorism division but as admin for three years. This she did but gained no sense of achievement, so Veronica applied to become an Armed Fire Officer.

She was accepted and excelled. The training had been thrilling. The test said that she was just the right person for the job. Her record stated that she was able to follow commands and take the initiative. She was 24, trained, willing and so excited. Although, for a whole year, all that training and experience was used to walk about at Heathrow Airport alongside a male officer. She had to ask herself whether that career officer had been right. She was bright and trained, willing and capable but was she here because they needed it to be a female? Veronica was bored.

The call for armed backup was received at 9:30am. She was not on duty but everyone else was dealing with a drone being flown over the airport. It was the 23rd of December and this was supposed to be her Christmas shopping day. She hadn't seen her parents for months and was planning a visit on Christmas Eve but when the call comes an officer must respond.

Veronica wanted to be annoyed because this was going to get in the way of her plans, but this was her first call out and she knew the exact protocol and procedure; and this wasn't Heathrow; the adrenaline rose and she was pumped.

It had taken the three of them twenty minutes to arrive at the shout; Darren the driver and Marcus, two tall and obviously physically strong AFOs. Another twenty minutes to assess the situation, speak to all concerned and put the appropriate cordons around the area. In this situation, she was in charge. Marcus and Darren were under her command and she loved it. This is what she had trained for and she was on automatic.

AFO Veronica Edwards had a job to do. Sort the outer cordon manned by local officers to prevent public access. Organise the evacuation of the housing estate, although there weren't many people at home on this estate at ten o'clock in the morning. Re-interview Julia to assess exactly what she had seen.

The inner cordon would consist of herself and the other two. They knew their roles. All three were armed.

Veronica's tactical boots and uniform were immaculate. There were no silver emblems, numbers, or buttons in this situation, but every piece of protective clothing was in place and ready. Everything fitted well.

The first job would be to light up the wood with floodlights facing directly at the identified zone. This would mean that her officers could not be seen behind the lights.

All the training had been using scenarios where the offender had been inside a house. This perpetrator was living in a wood, a small one, but it was challenging to tell where he was. The whole area was covered in building site debris.

She chose to be the marksman. Her shot was excellent, and her training had been thorough. They could not use tear gas in this situation as it would not be contained. She had considered the taser but they were not sure where he was and so they could not safely get close enough.

Julia had stated that he was near the abandoned cylindrical drainage pipe, so the working plan was to focus on that.

Julia was adamant that she had seen a handgun. She said that she had seen him waving it about. Veronica could see no reason for Julia to be mistaken. This was a real shout.

Plan in place, everyone ready.

Lights on!

. . .

Jake is screaming and swinging his arms.

I try to tell them to stay inside. We must stick together.

He has torn up a tree outside and is flinging excrement at the unseen intruders.

Charlie is chanting, "Run, run, run!"

Warren is squawking. "Go high my friend." But it was extremely difficult to think. The light is flooding directly into our home.

I can't leave them. I can't run. Who would care for them each night? Who will defend us if we are to be attacked? Could it be Stacey playing a trick? Questions are tumbling over each other not giving me enough time to think.

The light hurts my eyes, but I can see movement in areas around the beams. I push the others towards the back of our home. Jake has stopped screaming and returned to the comfort of Riley's arms. What should I do? Wait? Breathe slowly John. Focus on the brick John. Look at the word on the brick John.

I must protect my family. I have a right to protect my home.

Finally, the point of year 8! To learn about the rights, respects, and responsibilities of all citizens. Article 25 of the Universal Declaration of Human Rights: everyone has the right to a standard of living adequate for the health and wellbeing of himself and his family, including food, clothing, housing and medical care and necessary social services, and the right to security in the event of unemployment, sickness, disability, widowhood, old age or the lack of livelihood in circumstances beyond his control. On 10th December in 1948 the General Assembly of the United Nations adopted and proclaimed the Universal Declaration of Human Rights. I think that the United Nations signed it but perhaps the British have changed their minds.

Remembering this lesson was giving me clarity. We have a home and will defend it. Sir Coke said so.

. . .

Veronica has her gun focussed on the entrance of the tunnel. Darren will attempt to persuade the perpetrator to give himself up. Marcus is terrified and has finally decided to resign from the force but has been delegated 'by her' the job of staying in contact with the base.

Veronica lay on the ground, hidden from sight behind a light. This could mean promotion and out of Heathrow.

. . .

I am trying to put together all the social lessons I have been taught. I cannot go high because the others will be left behind. Piss myself and they will leave me alone? But no one is coming towards me. I have a poor record of rescues, but it is us who need rescuing. Do not tell the truth. Think, think, think John.

. . .

"Sir, he is speaking to others so we must assume they are hostages. Everything according to the book Sir. Repeating the request for the third time Sir. He has stopped throwing shit Sir."

"Veronica has him in her sights. Darren has asked him to throw out the gun toward the light and then to come out with his arms up Sir."

. . .

I risk moving towards the door. I am still not sure that they are talking to me so I must make sure that I check. No one has said John yet. I cannot see anyone due to the lights. Someone is shouting on my left about throwing a gun towards the lights.

The others are sobbing in the back room in a pile of arms and legs, fur, and skin. I will protect us, but I must make sure I understand the social situation. I slowly and silently rise from our doorway to stand in the light, my urban lilacs on my feet and the can opener in my hand.

"Put the gun down or we will shoot."

Everything has gone quiet. The same silence as the site machines make when they are turned off.

Veronica is totally focussed on the man in front of her. She moves her left foot for comfort.

(New boots squeak.)

I raise my arm to block out the light.
Veronica takes the shot.
Case closed.
Let the festivities begin.

Next Chance: LAC

"There will be a serious case review. All professionals will be required to make statements. All records will have to be read. We must leave no stone unturned. There will be a White Paper because of this one."

"We are not taking responsibility for this! We only knew him for a few months. No one could have predicted that this would happen! Surely no one individual can be accused of causing this!"

"The review will take months if not years, but we must look into all areas to ensure due diligence was always adhered to. After all, the child was a child in care, a Looked After Child. The responsibility of the local professionals."

"We don't use the term Looked After Child, or LAC as it has negative connotations, they lack for nothing. We prefer Child Looked After, CLA."

First Chance: ADD

"He doesn't have the described hyperactivity so it can't be ADHD. We always think that he is just Jamie. Please be kind to him. We love him very much. He won't be any trouble."

"Jamie, Jamie, James! I need to see your eyes so that I know you are listening."

(Surely, she means my ears?)

"I am looking for a word beginning with 'a'. Anyone?"

(Answered her own question.)

Theresa is an experienced teacher and up for promotion. This lesson observation is vital. She wants out of Reception Year. Under the table, Jamie is totally focussed as he creates a blue spiral of wax. But the young scientist must learn his phonics before he can learn about Archimedes; must he not?

(Will Jamie dumb down enough to consent to conform? He'll be choosing the biscuits before he knows it.)

Lightning Source UK Ltd.
Milton Keynes UK
UKHW040645011020
370850UK00003B/485

9 781839 752049